Family of Death

SANS SON

Family of Death

Six Generations of Executioners

GEOFFREY ABBOTT

Yeoman Warder (retired)
HM Tower of London

Illustrated by
JIL ATKINSON

ROBERT HALE · LONDON

© *Geoffrey Abbott 1995*
First published in Great Britain 1995

ISBN 0 7090 5591 9

Robert Hale Limited
Clerkenwell House
Clerkenwell Green
London EC1R 0HT

2 4 6 8 10 9 7 5 3 1

Photoset in Times by
Derek Doyle & Associates, Mold, Clwyd.
Printed in Great Britain by
St Edmundsbury Press Ltd, Bury St Edmunds, Suffolk.
Bound by WBC Book Manufacturers Limited,
Bridgend, Mid-Glamorgan.

Contents

Illustrations

Acknowledgements

Much credit is due to the many archivists, librarians and museum curators who so patiently aided my researches, not only in this country but also in France, Germany and Holland, and in particular to Dr Harold Hillman, Reader in Physiology, Director of Applied Neurobiology at the University of Surrey, for the clinical information he kindly provided.

Introduction

Just as in England, the sons of many French families follow the same profession as their fathers. They help out in the family shop, join the long established business, enlist in their father's regiment, a procedure accepted almost without question or hesitation by those involved, for what could be more natural than to follow in father's footsteps?

But what if those footsteps led, not to an honourable career in a city firm, the army or a bank, but to a way of life almost too horrific to contemplate? What if they were bloodstained footsteps, leading inexorably to the scaffold, there to whip and to maim, to brand and to burn, to bind and behead fellow members of the human race? A profession in which one would be a pariah, spurned and despised by all.

For such was the repugnance felt by the public at large towards executioners, so great was the stigma, that escape was almost impossible for him or indeed any member of the family. The sons were rarely if ever accepted into any other trade or business, and the daughters could only marry into the families of other executioners. And should an executioner have only daughters, a son-in-law was expected to succeed him. A race apart, executioners kept themselves to themselves in what was virtually a closed community.

Yet unbelievable as it may seem, this was the destiny of the Sansons, the dynasty of executioners who, for nearly two hundred years, carried out the sentences prescribed by the French courts, punishing criminals on behalf of the very society which nevertheless scorned the executioners themselves – a bitter irony indeed.

Nor was the task a sinecure, to be attended only occasionally. The earlier codes of justice carried a wide range of penalties. The edict promulgated by the Parliament of Paris in December 1666 condemned male gypsies to the galleys without trial and ordered that their womenfolk be flogged and banished; it declared war on persons without abode or work; it enforced regulations concerning gambling and smoking, and forbade the granting of asylum in noble houses to criminals.

Those guilty of such relatively minor transgressions as bigamy, blasphemy, cheating at cards, and petty theft, were subjected to public ignominy by a variety of devices. In the market-place the stocks secured the victims by the ankles, the pillory caged them like animals; the *carcan*, an iron collar, held the offender by means of a chain bolted to a stout post; placards proclaiming the victim's misdemeanours were displayed to passers-by, who seized the opportunity to shout abuse, or pelt the unfortunate miscreant with stones or even more obnoxious missiles.

A more severe punishment was that of being whipped through the streets by the executioner, the procession being led by a drummer lest the event should go unnoticed. Nagging or gossiping wives were shamed, if not permanently 'cured', by having to wear a scold's bridle, an iron cage locked about the head, incorporating a metal plate which, pressing down on the tongue, discouraged any inclination to protest. Neck pillories were much in vogue at one time, the victim being free to move about, albeit with neck and wrists secured in the holes of the wooden or iron device.

Many offences carried the penalty of branding, both men and women suffering as the executioner wielded the red-hot iron. In ancient times a fleur-de-lis design was burned into the victim's flesh, but this was later superseded by a series of letters and numbers depending on the crime and location of the prison.

For murderers, death by the rope, the sword or the dreaded wheel awaited, all being superseded from the end of the eighteenth century by the guillotine. To be hanged from the gallows, virtually death by strangulation, was the fate of the common criminal. Those of the upper classes were permitted the privilege of decapitation by the sword, a means of despatch usually, but not necessarily, more rapid and less painful than by the noose.

Being broken on the wheel was indisputably the most feared and the most barbaric. The victim was spreadeagled on a horizontally mounted cart-wheel, with his elbow and knee joints supported by the spokes. The executioner then methodically delivered violent blows with a thick iron bar, shattering in turn the criminal's arms above and below the elbows, the shins and the thigh bones. If previously sanctioned by the courts, a merciful end to the victim's hideous suffering would be brought about by the eventual application of the 'retentum', a heavy blow to the heart, or by the tightening of a thin cord around the victim's throat.

For even more heinous crimes, such as an assassination attempt on a royal personage, dire retribution awaited. Whether successful or not, the assassin was first interrogated by the *questionner*, the official torturer, in the presence of a judge who recorded the answers extracted. Reluctance to answer on the part of the suspect would be overcome by the administering of the water torture or the rack, which slowly and relentlessly dislocated the victim's joints; *estrapade*, a torture in which the victim, hands tied behind, was then hoisted off the floor by the wrists, resulting in appalling strain being imposed on the shoulder blades; and the 'boots', devices which could be tightened by means of a screw mechanism until the leg bones were crushed and splintered. Another version consisted of leather boots over which scalding water was poured, the shrinkage of the material causing excruciating agony.

Following the interrogation the now maimed and suffering felon was conveyed to the scaffold, there to keep his fatal rendezvous with the executioner. He too had his necessary appliances, a knife with which to amputate the hand that had struck the royal personage, and sulphur and molten lead to 'cauterize' the gaping wound. After the far from surgical operation, the victim was spreadeagled on the ground near the scaffold, his arms and legs roped to the harnesses of four strong horses. While the vast crowds watched, the steeds were lashed by the executioner's assistants, being driven off in opposite directions, thereby literally quartering the condemned felon.

Throughout the centuries the role of the French executioner was vital. His early title was that of 'Executioner

of High Justice', the distinction being that only high court judges and royal judges had the power to pass sentence of death. Before the Revolution of the late eighteenth century, he could not be nominated until ample information regarding his habits, conduct and piety had been submitted to the courts. Once accepted, he was considered a servant of the State, and held letters patent signed by the king. To show the distaste in which the office was held, even by those at the highest level, the documents of nomination were originally thrown on the table in the high chancellor's office for the executioner to pick up, but after 1645 the letters were given to him by hand.

As a rule he was not allowed to live in the town unless he

took up the official quarters, the 'house of pillory', so called because of the cage mounted on top in which offenders were confined for public opprobrium. In certain localities he wore a uniform consisting of a jacket emblazoned with the arms of the town and a ladder, symbolic of the method used at the gallows, whereby after the noose had encircled the victim's neck, the ladder on which he stood would be twisted to one side, thereby propelling him into the air. The back of the tunic bore a gibbet, the wooden post from the arm of which the cadaver was later suspended, there to swing until it disintegrated.

If the office of executioner during the earlier centuries was without respect or honour, it was, as compensation, invested with many perquisites. The main benefit was that granted by an Order of 1530 of *droit de havage*, whereby the executioner had the right to take a toll of the corn, fruit and merchandise offered for sale in the markets, to the amount which could be grasped in the hand (the actual amounts and commodities being detailed in the executioner's letter of appointment). This was a privilege designed to circumvent the problems he would have encountered in trying to buy goods, because many shopkeepers and others declined to receive money from hands such as his.

Even the *droit de havage* did not solve all the problems, for such was the aversion felt by the merchants, that the executioner or his assistants were made to take their entitlement not with the hand but with a tin spoon to avoid contaminating the rest of the goods. Disputes also arose when the vendors refused to allow the executioner to mark them on the arm with chalk, as was the custom, in order that those who had so unwillingly 'contributed' might be recognized.

In some districts the executioner was regarded with such disfavour that he could find neither a baker to sell him bread nor a landlord prepared to provide him with lodgings.

Sometimes extra perquisites were granted, one being the right to claim a part of the condemned person's clothing. At first only clothes below the waist were deemed his property, but eventually he could claim all the apparel. In some cities the executioner was also the knacker, skinning dead beasts and selling the skin and other remains, while elsewhere he was permitted to levy a tax on loose women! And should an executioner's assistant capture a stray pig, he could claim either its head or a sum of money in lieu.

All these perks were abolished in 1721, being replaced by an increase in his salary, but this increment hardly compensated for the expenses incurred by the executioner, for he had to supply and maintain the tumbrils (the carts which conveyed the doomed to the scaffold), horses and equipment, and pay the wages of this assistants. He was of course responsible for the upkeep of the guillotine and for buying the instruments and materials necessary for the various penalties – the pomade and gunpowder to apply to those he branded; shovels, tongs and bellows for the fire; fetters, straw, brooms, baskets and similar macabre sundries; even bran, sand and sawdust with which to soak up the blood which gushed across the boards after a decapitation.

This then was the way of life inherited by the Sanson dynasty, that of taking on the awesome task as the ultimate servant of the State, the final despatcher of the enemies of society. The eldest son of each generation succeeded to the office of executioner of Paris, and although other sons fulfilled the same role in provincial cities such as Reims, Provins, Tours, Auxerre, Montpellier, Blois, Rennes and Orléans, it was the capital city which, over the centuries, witnessed the Sansons administering justice and death, not only to the criminals of the day, but also to the hundreds of aristocrats and others who were guillotined during the French Revolution.

No other family in history has so completely committed so many of its members to preside over the scaffold, and the unique story of the six men who inherited the unenviable title of 'Monsieur de Paris' during the years 1688 to 1847 sheds new light on the capabilities and frailties of men subjected to the stress and strain of such an abhorrent occupation.

1 Origins of the Sansons

The roots of the Sansons are shrouded in the mists of time. Family legend has it that a Sanson held the post of Seneschal, steward of the household, to the Duke of Normandy, and joined the Crusades to the Holy Land; others bearing the same name were bannerets, senior knights, who accompanied William the Conqueror on his invasion of England in 1066.

Four centuries later a branch of the family had evidently established itself as municipal magistrates in Abbeville, Picardy, a descendent, Nicolas Sanson, achieving fame as one of the fathers of modern geography. It was even claimed that, during a royal visit to the town in 1638, King Louis XIII accepted Nicolas Sanson's hospitality, in marked contrast to the treatment a later king would receive at the hands of another Sanson a hundred and fifty or so years thereafter!

Whether these particular Sansons were the ancestors of those who are the subject of this book is open to conjecture. There is little doubt, however, that around the year 1600, a Sanson of Abbeville was appointed by the local lord of the château as his agent, with the duty of collecting revenues exacted from the inhabitants of Longueval (now Longeval), a village some fifty miles away. It was a profitable assignment, one third of the monies collected being retained as his own salary, and this income, together with lucrative ventures into the shipping business, made him a man of some substance, so much so, in fact, that he adopted the title 'Sanson de Longval'. And it was this worthy gentleman who was the progenitor of the succession of headsmen, the executioners who in the name of the law would punish and slay thousands of French citizens during the next two centuries.

Sanson de Longval married a Mademoiselle Brossier, and they had two sons – Jean-Baptiste, born in 1624, and Charles, in 1635. Both the parents died in an epidemic while the younger boy was still a baby, but their uncle, Pierre Brossier, a magistrate and wealthy landowner of Limeuse, a nearby town, adopted the two orphaned lads, treating them with the kindness and affection he showed towards his own daughter Colombe, a girl the same age as Charles.

The three children grew up together and, on reaching his early thirties, Jean-Baptiste studied law, qualifying to become a magistrate. Charles, almost constantly in Colombe's company, inevitably fell in love with her, sentiments which she reciprocated. But their romantic dreams came to naught when Pierre Brossier announced that not only had he used his influence to have Jean-Baptiste appointed a Councillor of the Court of Abbeville, but it was also his wish that the young man should marry Colombe forthwith.

In those days, in which the father's word was law, no argument was tolerated, no appeal considered. The wedding duly took place, and Charles, grief-stricken, joined the King's service and sailed for Canada. There, with the musketeers, he took part in the fighting against rebellious colonists and Indians, remaining in that country for three years until eventually he returned to France.

Disembarking in Toulon, he made his way to Abbeville, where he found that disaster had overtaken Jean-Baptiste and his wife. Pierre Brossier had died, and the family estates had been taken over by the local landowner. The subsequent legal wrangles had drained his brother's resources, the strain proving so great that Jean-Baptiste had suffered a stroke and was now paralysed and blind. Charles, realizing their plight, immediately put much of his savings at their disposal. Seeing Colombe again had awakened all the love he had felt for her, but as the months passed he also realized that he could not expect her to break her marriage vows; accordingly, in 1661, he left for Dieppe, forty miles away. The barracks there housed the regiment of the Marquis de la Boisserie and, as was the practice in many countries at that time, he purchased a lieutenant's commission in the regiment. He took part in the battle of Gravelines with his troops and during the campaign earned a reputation for courage and strong leadership.

He continued to support Colombe and his ailing brother financially and wrote many letters, but did not trust himself to visit them. However the situation changed radically when, on 31 May 1662, he received an urgent letter from Colombe. His brother Jean-Baptiste had died, his creditors had seized the house and all its contents after the funeral, and Colombe was even then *en route* for Dieppe, and was lodging in the village of Envermeu a few miles away.

Instantly Charles saddled his horse and rode to meet her. After a touching reunion the young couple set off back to Dieppe, Colombe clinging behind him on the steed, both doubtlessly looking forward to a happy future, together at last. But once again fate was to intervene, for as they rode along a violent storm suddenly erupted. There was a blinding flash of lightning, a momentous act of nature which was to change the lives of so many people for generations to come, for the startled horse reared wildly, and threw both its riders to the ground.

Charles fell heavily and lost consciousness. When he recovered some time later, it was to find himself being cared for by a young woman and a couple who were evidently her parents. Sadly, they told him that Colombe had been killed, but that he was not badly injured and would recover.

His grief was somewhat alleviated by the care and tenderness shown by the girl in ministering to his wounds, and it was not long before love blossomed between the handsome Charles de Longval and his attractive nurse, whose name, he had established, was Marguerite Jouenne. So strong was her affection for him that she even consented to become his mistress, yet inexplicably she rejected his many proposals of marriage.

Fully recovered, Charles rejoined his regiment in Dieppe, yet could not get Marguerite out of his mind. Despite the surly reception he always received from her father he continued to visit her, yet each time she spurned his fervent pleas that they should wed, albeit accompanied by tears.

But it was not until weeks later that the reason for her refusals became horrifyingly clear. One day, whilst crossing the main square in Dieppe, he noticed a public execution taking place on the scaffold. Not a rare sight, and hardly one to attract his attention; yet as he passed he stopped short, as, almost unbelievingly, he recognized the executioner as being none other than Pierre Jouenne, Marguerite's father! And such was the abhorrence which he, like most people, felt towards the members of that profession, that Charles realized the inevitability of the situation. He would have to give her up.

So strong was his affection for Marguerite, however, that it proved impossible. Time and time again he found himself drawn back to her family's house, the grim meaning of its name now horrifyingly clear to him; *Le Clos Maudit*, The Accursed Enclosure.

Gossip of the liaison soon spread around the barracks, and eventually reached the ears of his commanding officer, the Marquis de la Boisserie. Infuriated that one of his officers should associate with an executioner's family and thereby besmirch the honour of the regiment, the marquis ordered Charles to cease seeing Marguerite, or be dismissed from the service.

Torn between love and duty, Charles rode to *Le Clos Maudit*, hoping that by seeing Marguerite just once more he could decide what to do. At the secluded house he found a furious row in progress. Pierre had discovered that his daughter had a lover and, incensed, was threatening to kill her with the beheading sword if she refused to name him. He knew she had not been meeting another executioner's son, and who among his own profession would want her now, a virgin no longer?

Seeing Pierre's almost insane determination to kill his daughter should she not divulge the truth, Charles's mind was made up. Frantically he intervened, swearing that he loved Marguerite, and was prepared to marry her – even though it meant accepting Pierre's ultimatum that by doing so he would have to follow his father-in-law's profession and eventually succeed him on the scaffold.

That resolved, Charles returned to Dieppe, there to resign his commission by breaking his sword, and shortly afterwards the now happy couple were married.

All these events were described by him in a document written in archaic French some thirty years later, in which he expressed regret to his successors for the career to which he had condemned them:

> God, in His infinite goodness, measured on our shoulders the cross He wished us to bear; there is no misfortune, however heavy, to which one cannot be reconciled. And what at first appears to us as impossible for a man to accomplish, as it is for him to swallow all the waters of the ocean, comes to pass by the mere strength of habit.
>
> After entering into rebellion against my fate, I have been led to suffer patiently the evil I did not deserve, as well as the consequences of my imprudence, praying that my death should be less tainted than my life. But although children only subsist by the will of their parents, although they owe to them life and education, I apprehend that mine, before the singular difference they must find between their existence and that which they had a right to hope for at my hands, will murmur against their father; and before asking for God's mercy, I wish to confess my sins, and to state the reasons that led me to adopt the miserable profession of executioner, so that they may forgive me, if I deserve forgiveness.
>
> Signed, Charles Sanson, Thursday the eleventh day of December, in the year of our Lord one thousand six hundred and ninety-three.

That Pierre wasted little time in introducing Charles to his new way of life was evidenced by official records which stated 'that having to break on the wheel a certain Martin Eslau, Master Pierre Jouenne, principal executioner, compelled his son-in-law, who was but lately married, to aim a blow at the culprit. But he, the said son-in-law, fell in a fit, and was hooted by the mob'.

By that time Charles had developed into a big muscular man with long blond hair. One account describes him as wearing a woollen shirt, leather knee breeches and heavy boots, garments essential when employed on the scaffold, and doubtless protected by the almost mandatory leather apron. He had always been a pious and God-fearing man, and doubtless his faith, and the devotion of his wife, supported him in his new role. That the task was repellent to him was evidenced by his morose and sad expression, and the future must have seemed bleak indeed. His morale suffered a further blow when, in 1681, Marguerite died giving birth, though the baby, a boy, survived. Soon after that sad event his father-in-law passed away, Charles then assuming the mantle of chief executioner.

By now he had learned the skills of the scaffold, carrying out the sentences of the court by branding, whipping, even breaking victims on the wheel. One so despatched was a murderer and thief, Claude Vautier, in 1685. To a great extent, Charles had not only mentally insulated himself against the horrors of inflicting the punishments but seemed also to have bowed to the inevitability of his fate, to the extent that when, in 1687, the office of executioner in Paris became vacant, he applied for it.

The vacancy arose when Nicolas Levasseur, the current executioner of that city, was relieved of his post for some minor lapse of duty. Like Marguerite, Levasseur's wife belonged to the Jouenne family, whose members had for many years supplied the towns of Normandy with executioners, but their hopes that one of her male relatives might be considered for the vacancy were dashed, due to the price demanded by the outgoing headsman.

The prestigious post of 'Monsieur de Paris' was much sought after among those of the profession, the number of punishments and executions in the capital city guaranteeing a considerable increase in the executioner's income. However several hurdles had to be surmounted before being appointed. The King himself had to approve of his character and record of ability on the scaffold and, just as in purchasing a commission in the army, so the would-be headsman had to raise the large sum of money demanded by the retiring incumbent who sought to recoup the price he originally had to pay (this custom incidentally was also practised by those desirous of becoming yeoman warders of the Tower of London; should the incumbent die in office, however, the money went to the Constable of the Tower, giving rise to the saying, 'May you never die a yeoman warder!').

In addition the Treasury required a registration fee of 6,000 livres for the 'Lettre de Provision', the letter of appointment signed by the King. The document which appointed Charles Sanson as 'Monsieur de Paris' in 1688 has survived to this day in the French National Archives, and is quoted here in full.

> Louis, by the grace of God King of France and Navarre, to all those who shall see these presents, greetings!
>
> By the order of our Court of the Parlement of Paris, the eleventh August of the present year, it having been ordained, with a view to the uninterrupted trial of cases, that Charles Sanson known as Longval shall alone fulfil the office of Executioner of High Justice in our city, provostry and viscounty of Paris, subject to his obtaining our letters patent for the said office; wherefore be it known that in view of the good account given us of the said Charles Sanson known as Longval, we have, in accordance with the said order, given and granted, and do by these presents give and grant him the status of Executioner of the High Works and Criminal Sentences in our aforesaid city, provostry and viscounty of Paris, heretofore held and exercised by Nicolas Levasseur, last incumbent thereof, the same having been discharged by the said order of our said Court of Parlement of Paris, and added, under the counterseal of our Chancery, in respect of the said office and its tenure, future exercise, enjoyment and use by the aforesaid Sanson, to the rights of levy in the fairs and markets of our said city, provostry and viscounty of Paris, products, gains, revenues and emoluments, such and similar as have well and properly been enjoyed by the incumbents of like offices; to wit; enjoyment of the house and habitation of the *Pillori des Halles*, its appurtenances and dependencies without let or hindrance for whatsoever cause, and furthermore the right to exact from each merchant bearing eggs on his back or by hand, one egg, from each saddle-load two eggs, from each cart-load a demi-quarteron, and from each basket of apples, pears, grapes and other produce, whether arriving by land or by water in boats carrying the same load as a horse, one sou; for each laden horse the same amount, and for each cart, two sous; for those bringing whether by land or by water, green peas, medlars, hemp-seed, mustard seed, poulavin, millet, walnuts, chestnuts, hazelnuts, his spoonful as has always been the custom; from each itinerant merchant bringing on

his back or by hand, butter, cheese, poultry and fresh-water fish, six deniers; for each horse one sou; for each cart-load of beans, two sous; for each tip-cart twenty sous and a carp; and for each bag of peas or broad beans in pods, one sou; and for each basket, six deniers; and for each case of oranges and lemons brought in by itinerant merchants either by water or by land, one sou; for each wagon-load of oysters in the shell, one quarteron and for each boat-load in proportion, and for every person bringing brooms, one broom; for every horse-load, two; and for every cart-load, six brooms. For every merchant bringing in coal, his potful; from sworn rope makers, rope for the executions, all of which rights have been levied both in our own city of Paris and in other parts of our Kingdom, which the said Sanson will enjoy, as also exemption from all levies in respect of nightwatch, guards, bridges, ferries, receipt of wine and other beverages for his own provender, with the right to carry arms both offensive and defensive, himself and his servants, on account of his office.

We hereby command the Provost of Paris or his deputy at the criminal court of the Chatelet in the said town, after assuring himself of the virtuous life and morals, and the Catholic, Apostolic, and Roman religion of the said Sanson, and administering to him the customary oath required in such cases, to place and establish him in our name, in the possession and enjoyment of the said office, together with the rights and exemptions above mentioned, completely and peaceably ending and causing to cease all disturbances and obstacles raised in opposition, and seeing that he is obeyed and listened to by all whom it may concern in matters touching and regarding the said office.

In witness of which we have caused our seal to be attached these presents.

Bestowed at Versailles, the twenty-third day of September in the year of grace sixteen eighty-eight, and of our reign the forty-sixth, and signed on the fold, in the King's Name.

The official residence mentioned in that historic document was *La Maison du Pillori des Halles*, the House of Pillory, a gloomy, octagonal-shaped building, on top of which was mounted a revolving cage, rotated at intervals by the executioner's assistants, in which victims were displayed for the public's edification, the offenders having a notice about their necks proclaiming their crime. The house was in the market area and so was surrounded by stalls and shops, whilst adjoining the residence was a stable and sheds, one of the latter being used to store the decapitated bodies of those executed until their burial the following day.

The fact that this morgue was at his disposal led Charles to experiment, to study anatomy and buy medical books, a pursuit indulged in by most of his successors. So practised did he become as the months passed that not only did he become proficient at setting broken bones, but even concocted medicines and healing balms for common ailments, with which he cured those whose pains outweighed their distaste for one of his profession.

His son Charles, known in the family as Charles II, was now seven years of age. A bright, intelligent boy, he was deprived of anything resembling normal schooling or even playmates of his own age, the aura of the scaffold deterring potential companions. His father engaged a priest to impart the basic rudiments of reading and writing, mathematics and of course some religious instruction to the lad.

He also bought a house near the church of Saint Laurent, a retreat in which to spend his off-duty hours with his son, away from the hubbub of the market, the parading of the miscreants and the accompanying abuse of the mob, which at times made life in the *Pillori des Halles* almost intolerable.

When on duty, Sanson wore his official uniform, royal blue breeches and a red shirt, embroidered on the chest with the gallows in black, and the fateful ladder portrayed across the shoulders, together with a wide-brimmed hat and heavy shoes. This apparel was in almost daily use for, not unnaturally in a city the size of Paris, scaffold business was brisk. Bigamists of either sex had to be whipped in public, much to the delight of the avidly watching crowds. Prostitutes received the same treatment, convicted bank-rupts and other offenders being pilloried and branded. And of course there were occasional executions, including that of Jean Nouis, broken on the wheel for theft and murder, and later a 21-year-old youth, François Mannequin, for giving false evidence. Nor were women exempt. Charles executed

Gabrielle Henry, wife of Major Jacques Piedeseigle, guilty of murder; Clare Lermenet for theft 'after horrible torture', and in 1691 he despatched Urbaine Attibard, aged thirty-five who, having poisoned her husband, had been sentenced to 'have her fist cut off, to be then hanged, her body to be burned and her ashes scattered to the wind'.

Perhaps the case which brought him most publicity, welcome or not, occurred in 1699, and involved a ravishingly beautiful woman named Angelique Carlier. This marriageable lady, the daughter of a wealthy printer and bookbinder of Metz, was much sought after by the rich landowners of France but, persuaded by her aunt, she rejected their advances and instead married M. Ticquet, a magistrate and councillor of Parliament. This gentleman soon realized that his wife had very expensive tastes, much money being required to maintain her string of carriages, her teams of horses, and to maintain her position as one of the leading lights of Parisian fashionable society.

So different were their natures, so violent the arguments, that whatever affection there had been turned to hatred. Angelique took a lover, M. de Montgeorges, a dashing captain in the French Guards, and made no secret of the affair, the gossip making her cuckolded husband the laughing stock of the city. Not content with that, Angelique determined to rid herself of the man who thwarted her every ambition. Accordingly she planned to have him murdered.

She employed Jacques Moura, her porter, as her chief accomplice, telling him to recruit others in readiness. But then, after second thoughts, she called off the plan, preferring instead to poison her husband by preparing a cup of broth and ordering his valet to take it to his room. However the loyal servant's suspicions were aroused by this seemingly solicitous deed by a woman whose motives he suspected, and so he deliberately dropped the cup, spilling its contents.

At the frustration of her scheme, Angelique decided to act. A few nights later, as M. Ticquet was returning home, shots suddenly rang out and he fell, having been hit by five bullets, none however proving fatal.

A criminal investigation immediately followed, and while the perpetrators of the attack could not be identified, those

involved in the earlier conspiracy were apprehended, the two prime suspects being Jacques Moura, the porter, and Angelique Ticquet herself. Following the trial, the sentence passed by the court on 3 June 1699 'condemned Angelique-Nicole Carlier to be decapitated in the Place de Grève; Jacques Moura, her late porter to be hanged; their property to be confiscated, and from Angelique's property ten thousand livres for the benefit of the King, and one hundred thousand livres for that of Ticquet, her husband, to be extracted'.

The compensation for her husband was increased to 120,000 livres by order of Parliament, but no appeal was allowed against the death sentence, even though the victim had survived the attack.

Mme Ticquet was led to the torture chamber by the Criminal Lieutenant Deffita, one of her former admirers, and the sentence read out to her. She was then urged by the lieutenant to divulge the names of all her accomplices. When she refused, she was subjected to the water torture, being strapped to a bench, a cow horn then inserted in her mouth. A wooden bucket full of water stood nearby, but after the first jugful had been poured down her throat she capitulated, and confessed everything.

On the scaffold, meanwhile, awaited not one Charles but two, Monsieur de Paris having sent for his son, who had been learning the ropes, in more ways than one, under the tuition of the executioner of Pontoise. At last they saw the procession with its armed escort, wending its way through the immense crowds. Angelique, clad in a white gown, was accompanied in the tumbril by her fellow conspirator Jacques Moura and her confessor, the Abbé de la Chetardie.

Even as the doleful procession halted, a violent storm broke over the city. Spectators ran for shelter beneath balconies and in doorways; Charles senior stayed with Angelique, conscious that his usual composure was slipping away, his nerves raw as the thunder and the nearness of the beautiful woman evoked memories of the death of Colombe. Delay was unavoidable, for he dared not risk slipping on the wet scaffold boards while wielding the heavy execution sword; so executioner and victims had perforce to sit for half an hour in sight of the scaffold and the hearse which was waiting in readiness for Angelique's corpse.

At last the rain eased off. Jacques Moura was the first to be despatched, and then Sanson helped the woman to ascend the steps. As he did so, Angelique raised his hand and kissed it, grateful for the solicitude he had shown her. This touching gesture proved too much for Sanson. Turning to his son he exclaimed, 'Take my place! My strength is failing me!'

Dutifully if not willingly, the younger man stepped forward, and waited until Angelique had prayed. Then as she asked, 'Sir, will you be good enough to show me the position I am to take?' he answered, 'Kneel down with your head up; lift your hair away from your neck and falling forward over your face.'

Charles II stepped back and gripped the heavy, two-handed sword. Reports had it that even as he made the preliminary swing to gain the necessary momentum with the weapon, Angelique, utterly feminine to the end, exclaimed, 'Be sure not to disfigure me!' the interruption causing the young executioner to falter. Whether the reason was distraction or inexperience, the sword merely slashed across the side of the woman's neck, the crowd gasping in horror on seeing the blood flowing from the gaping wound – yet the head did not fall! Charles II struck again, the blade hissing through the air; but still her head remained attached to her body. Finally, as described in the family's memoirs, 'Blinded by the blood which spurted at every stroke, Charles brandished the weapon a third time with a kind of frenzy. At last the head rolled at his feet. His assistants picked it up; and several witnesses asserted that even in death it retained its former calmness and beauty.'

That very night Charles Sanson, Monsieur de Paris, overwhelmed by the horrors of his profession, resigned his post in favour of his son, although he himself would still have to legalize executions by his presence on the scaffold.

Needing a partner in his approaching old age – he was now sixty-four – Charles the elder married again, less than a month after the appalling débâcle on the scaffold. On 11 July 1699, in the church of Notre-Dame de Bonne Nouvelle, he married Jeanne-Renee Dubut, a placid, religious woman, the elder daughter of Pierre Dubut, a master turner who lived nearby. But despite the love and care lavished on him by his wife, he was unable to shake off his obsessions. He became uneasy, and started at the slightest sound. Darkness filled him with such terror that a lighted lantern was kept burning at his bedside. Even his hobby of medicine proved no palliative, for the sight of a drop of blood threw him into nervous convulsions, the intensity of which appalled all those who witnessed them.

Hoping that a complete change of surroundings might help, in 1703 he and Jeanne-Renee moved to a small farm at

Condé, in the Brie district, but his health continued to fail and four years later, in May 1707, he died.

His body was brought back to Paris, the funeral being held in the church of Saint Laurent. Hundreds of mourners attended, among them councillors and magistrates, merchants and traders; those he had impressed by his gentle and humane character, those he had healed with his unguents.

After the service the remains of the man who had performed over a hundred executions and who, through love of a woman, had founded generations of executioners to come, was buried within the church, his coffin next to that of his beloved Colombe, his passing mourned by all who had known him.

2 Charles Sanson II

When Charles the elder resigned in May 1699, he was nevertheless responsible for all executions performed on the Paris scaffold, although it was his son who positioned the noose, swung the sword and wielded the iron bar. However, when Charles retired to his farm at Condé four years later, the young man assumed full responsibility with effect from 3 September 1703. Now 22 years of age, with several years' experience behind him, he had got over the trauma of the Ticquet affair and was now a fully fledged executioner. Competent and efficient, he continued to deal satisfactorily with the common criminals who mounted the scaffold steps – thieves, highway robbers, murderers and similar male-factors.

Being a dutiful and loving son, he frequently visited the family home, noting with dismay his father's steadily deteriorating health. But someone else monopolized his affections, for on 30 April 1707, eight days before his father passed away, Charles, now twenty-six, married Anne-Marthe Dubut, his stepmother's sister, an attractive, strong-minded girl just two years younger than himself. Oddly, the relationship thus formed meant that his stepmother was also his sister-in-law, and his wife was also his step-aunt!

The wedding took place in the church of Notre-Dame de Bonne Nouvelle. Anyone who was anyone in scaffold circles was present; relatives of the happy couple, executioners from provincial towns, even officials of the judiciary attended, to give their blessings to bride and groom.

Like his father, Charles was of a mild and gentle disposition, inclined to show mercy to his victims wherever possible. Either because of some fatalistic quirk of his

29

nature, or because he had been brought up in a way of life
totally dominated by the scaffold, he took it for granted that
he too should be an executioner.

In 1716 the Sansons had a daughter, Anne-Renee, who
later was to marry one Chretien Zelle, a musician. Lest it
should be thought that she had thereby escaped the stigma
of her family's profession, it should be pointed out that
THEIR descendants became executioners of Soissons!

Within the next few years Charles and Anne-Marthe had
two more children, both boys. The eldest, Charles-
Jean-Baptiste (whom henceforth I shall refer to as
Jean-Baptiste, to avoid further confusion) was born in Paris
on 19 April 1719 and was inevitably destined to succeed his
father's position in society. His younger brother, born two
years later, was also a 'Charles', being christened Nicolas
Charles Gabriel. On reaching maturity, he became
executioner of Reims, and was succeeded by his son
Jean-Louis in 1770, who in turn held the post until dying in
1794. His father outlived him, passing away in the following
year, and so, except for one brief episode, he exits from our
story of the family.

The ancient records fail to list the hundreds of
punishments meted out to the petty criminals of the day or
the executions which were performed by Charles Sanson.
Highlights however were not omitted, one of the most
gruesome and bizarre being the affair involving Comte
Antoine-Joseph de Horn, grandson of the Prince de Ligne
and cousin of the Regent.

It took place in 1720, at a time when the financial affairs of
the country were in turmoil and panicking investors were
withdrawing their capital from the banks. Amid all the news
of falling profits and the activities of speculators, the
announcement that the 22-year-old Comte de Horn, a scion
of the highest ranks of Paris society, had been arrested for
murder, came like a bombshell. But the facts were
indisputable. He, together with an accomplice, the
Chevalier de Milhe, in attempting to rob a man of 100,000
livres under the pretext of buying shares, had fatally stabbed
him. The murder had taken place in a tavern on the rue
Quincampoix, both men had been arrested, and de Milhe had
confessed that the attack had been planned beforehand. The

comte himself claimed as a mitigating factor that the murdered man was a Jew.

The royal court was, not unnaturally, shocked and horrified that someone as high-born as a relative of the Regent should be involved in such a sordid crime, and when the judge pronounced that the two murderers were to be broken on the wheel, petitions for clemency on behalf of de Horn were signed by such dignitaries as Prince Claude de Ligne, the Marquis d'Harcourt, the Earl of Egmont, the Archbishop of Cambrai, the Princesse de Gonzague and others of similar ilk. It was claimed in mitigation that insanity ran in his family, that two of his uncles and his grandfather were mentally deranged; even that his father was mad. But the high-ranking deputation which assembled at the Palais Royal received short shrift from the Regent; despite being related to the comte through his mother, the Princess Palatine, reprieve was out of the question. Justice must be done, although he intimated that commutation of the sentence to that of being decapitated by the sword would be considered, and moreover that the venue for the execution would be private, held in the prison courtyard.

The leader of the deputation, the Marquis de Creqy, one of the godsons of King Louis XIV, was so convinced that the sword would be used that he visited Charles Sanson, and begged him to be as merciful as possible; to uncover only the neck of the victim, and not to strike until de Horn had received absolution. He also asked Sanson to obtain a silk-lined coffin wherein the corpse could be taken for burial, Charles willingly acceding to these doleful requests.

Rumour had it that the executioner also had another visitor, a lady heavily veiled, who pleaded with Charles to allow the comte to escape. This lady then revealed herself to be none other than the Comtesse de Parabere, the Regent's mistress – and de Horn's paramour! Upon Charles explaining that this was impossible, that there would be a strong guard of soldiers, the comtesse went further, offering him not only money and jewels, but even herself! Sanson's reactions to such an offer are not recorded, but as a man of honour, with a strong sense of duty, all he could promise was that, should a rescue attempt be made by de Horn's supporters, he, Sanson, would not resist them. Moreover, he promised, he would obtain some souvenir of the comte for the comtesse.

Shortly after the two visits, the executioner received instructions to collect his victims at six o'clock the next morning from the torture chamber and convey them, not to the privacy of the prison yard but to the Place de Grève, where, in public, he was to break them on the wheel; the Regent had not kept his word. Worse was to follow, for the sentence did not authorize Sanson to administer the retentum, the eventual strangling of the victim which would bring an end to his suffering.

As ordered, Charles and his assistants collected their victims from the Conciergerie prison. Both men had been subjected to torture by the 'boots', their legs having been so badly maimed that they had to be assisted into the tumbril, and on arrival at the Place de Grève, the executioner took de Horn in his arms and carried him up the steps to the scaffold.

Positioned thereon were two horizontally mounted wheels, each having had planks in the shape of a St Andrew's Cross secured to them. The two men were duly roped, spreadeagled, to the crosses, and after prayers had been said by the accompanying priest, the execution commenced. Sanson, however, was determined to be as merciful as he dared. He handed the heavy iron bar to his chief assistant Nicolas Gros and, despite not having received the necessary authority, surreptitiously slipped a thin cord about the comte's throat and tightened it. Positioning himself between the body and the court official who, from a distance, was supervising the executions, he stepped back and watched Nicolas Gros deliver blows to what was already a lifeless corpse.

The chevalier, meanwhile, was uttering screams of agony as the other assistant swung the iron bar at his limbs, shattering each in turn. In vain the priest wiped the perspiration from the victim's brow and forced a few drops of water into his gaping mouth, until at last Sanson, struck by the inequality of the suffering of the two men, ordered Gros to deliver the *coup de grâce*, the blow to the chest which would end the man's life.

Shortly after the execution, a carriage drawn by six

horses, preceded by a mounted attendant and followed by six servants in magnificent livery, entered the square. Next came other carriages, all draped in black, as were the horses themselves. From one emerged the figure of the Marquis de Creqy. He wore the uniform of a colonel-general and Inspector of the King's Army, and wore the insignias of the Golden Fleece, and the Grand Crosses of Saint Louis and Saint Jean of Jerusalem. Approaching the scaffold he reminded the executioner of his promise to be merciful. Sanson replied, 'Monseigneur, at eight o'clock this morning, M. le Comte de Horn was dead, and the bar wielded by my assistant struck a dead body.' The Marquis, his tones showing his relief, exclaimed, 'Well, our house shall remember that if it could obtain nothing from the clemency of the Regent and from the justice of Parliament, it is at least indebted to the humanity of the executioner.'

The comte's body was untied and taken to one of the carriages. It was so mutilated that the limbs seemed ready to separate from the trunk, one of the legs only adhering to the body by a shred of skin. The carriage drove to a nearby chapel, where the remains were placed on a bier, and Masses were said for the dead. Later that evening an envelope was delivered to the Comtesse de Parabere. It contained a lock of Antoine de Horn's hair.

The fever of excitement engendered by the comte's execution had hardly died down when, on 15 October of the following year, 1721, the capture of Cartouche was announced by the police. Cartouche, the criminal who had carried out so many audacious robberies, who had eluded and defied the authorities for so long, whose gangs had raided banks, shops and châteaux, had waylaid carriages, caravans and pedestrians, had finally been brought to book.

Louis Dominique Cartouche, gang leader, bandit and pickpocket *extraoardinaire*, fifty-eight years old, illiterate yet possessed of much native cunning, had been sought after for more than ten years. Almost a legend in his time, he was said to possess almost hypnotic powers over women, despite Sanson's description of him; 'Only four and a half feet tall, but his thinness made him look taller than he really was; his head between the ears was exceedingly developed, his hair was thin and shaggy, and the eye not wanting in malice. It was surprising that a man so ugly should be represented as a lady-killer.'

Again and again Cartouche had displayed his contempt for the law, until eventually secret orders for his capture went out, and a spy, Duchatelet, infiltrated his network. Finally he was reported to be in hiding at a wine dealer's at La Courtelle.

M. le Blanc, the Secretary of State for War, took personal command of the operation and with forty armed soldiers and policemen, raided the house. They found Cartouche in bed, six loaded pistols on the table beside him and, overpowering him, they took him to the Chatelet prison, where he was chained to a stone pillar, the triple doors of his cell being guarded by four men.

Not that the Chatelet could hold him. A cell-mate happened to be a mason and, freeing each other, they dug down into the floor and dropped into a large sewer. Wading through the foul-smelling outflow, they broke through a wall and found themselves in the cellar of a greengrocer's shop. On mounting the steps, they disturbed a dog, whose barking alerted the owner of the shop. He, sympathetic to the convicts, would have allowed them to escape, but a passing police patrol came in and, recognizing Cartouche by the chains still attached to his wrists and ankles, took him back to his cell. Following this daring attempt, he was transferred to the main prison, the Conciergerie.

There he was visited by Charles Sanson. On seeing him, Cartouche, with a flash of humour, pointed to the executioner's stick and asked if he had brought it to take his measure. But the gangleader's insouciance faded when, on 26 November 1721, he and five members of his gang were sentenced to be broken on the wheel, after first enduring the *question ordinaire et extraordinaire* in the torture chamber.

The next day, crippled after suffering the agony of the 'boots', Cartouche was taken to the Place de Grève through streets lined with jeering crowds. The square itself was packed, a contemporary journal describing how 'All night long carriages carried passengers to the Place, until it was jammed with people, all waiting for the event. Windows facing the square were lit all night. The cold was biting, but the crowd lit fires right in the square, and local merchants

sold food and drink. Everyone was laughing, drinking, singing. Most of the spectators had had their places reserved for over a month.'

During the journey Cartouche showed signs of agitation, and when he saw the dreaded wheel he turned pale, beads of sweat forming on his brow. He no longer made a show of his cynicism, although when he was secured to the 'Croix de St André' and the first blow was struck, he exclaimed loudly 'One!' But as the iron bar continued to descend on his limbs, he lapsed into silence.

Even for one whose crimes had been of such magnitude, the benefit of the retentum had been included in the sentence. However due to an error by the clerk of the court, Charles Sanson was not informed. The sickening procedure was therefore carried out in full. Cartouche received eleven blows of the iron bar, and was still just alive twenty minutes after being placed on the wheel.

Nor was that the end of the affair. Minor members of the gang were 'induced' to confess before they too were strapped to the wheel, these admissions bringing about the arrests of scores of others, including a whole network of accomplices and informers, receivers of stolen goods, 'reputable' jewellers, even police officers. By the following June a hundred and fifty felons were incarcerated in the prisons, most of them eventually being executed for their complicity in the long series of crimes.

Among those despatched were five of Cartouche's mistresses who were duly hanged in turn on Sanson's scaffold. Even the arch-criminal's young brother, scarcely fifteen years of age, was not only sentenced to hard labour for life, but also 'to be suspended under the armpits for two hours in the Place de Grève'. This peculiar punishment had been devised by the instructing judge, M. Arnould de Boueix whose father, a criminal lieutenant (police officer) had recently been murdered on the highway.

Sanson's assistants suspended the young lad as ordered, but the victim soon started shrieking that he would rather die than endure such pain. Charles, never having had to administer such a punishment before, and therefore unaware of its possible consequences, was nonplussed. But on seeing that the youngster's face was growing red and he could no longer speak, the executioner disregarded the possibility that the boy might be exaggerating his complaints, and ordered that the victim be freed, although the two hours stipulated were far from expired. Cut down, the boy was taken back to the prison, but sadly died without regaining consciousness.

Away from the scaffold, Charles was encountering financial difficulties. In October 1721 the authorities had abolished the *droit de havage*, the lucrative perquisites of the profession, and had replaced it by a far from adequate increase in salary. Further prolonged negotiations brought the concession whereby executioners could retain all the victims' clothing, instead of only that below the waist, as previously. A bonus of five sous per execution was also paid, a rate deemed derisory by the profession. In order to supplement his salary Charles developed his knowledge of medicine, providing pills and ointments for those in need, at a price.

Over the next year or so, Sanson's health started to fail, although he was only forty-five years old. On 24 May 1726, despite his weak condition, he responded to the call of duty when a man named Etienne Benjamin des Chauffours was sentenced to death by burning, having been found guilty of committing homosexual crimes. As a search of his residence revealed a list incriminating over two hundred others, mostly aristocrats, a reprieve was out of the question, so as a deterrent only the procurer was put to the flames, though he was permitted the benefit of the retentum before the fires devoured him.

In August 1726 Charles Sanson submitted his resignation. Now a very sick man, he was nevertheless determined that his eldest son Jean-Baptiste should follow the family tradition, even though the boy was but seven years old. His wife Anne-Marthe summoned a notary from the Chatelet prison to draw up a legal document to transfer the appointment, and two of Charles's friends, *questionaires* named Georges Herisson and François Prud'homme, to act as witnesses.

The two men were also asked whether they would train the boy, while performing the actual duties themselves, until he had reached the age of eighteen, when he could then take the oath of office as Executioner of Judgements and Criminal Sentences. Until such time he would of course have to be present at executions in order to legalize the proceedings. Both consented, though Herisson, who had been executioner and torturer to Parliament from 1715 to 1717, left some time later to become executioner of Melun.

Charles Sanson died on 12 September 1726, and was buried in the family tomb in the church of Saint Laurent. As at the funeral of his father, scores of mourners attended the funeral service, a fitting tribute to a man who had achieved so much in tempering justice with mercy.

After a respectable period of mourning, his widow Anne-Marthe married again. True to the family traditions which she had always guarded so jealously, the man she chose was Jean-Baptiste Barre, one of the torturers employed by Parliament!

3   Charles-Jean-Baptiste

As mentioned in the last chapter, this member of the Sanson family will be referred to as Jean-Baptiste, to avoid confusion.

The death of Charles Sanson could well have broken the fateful chain of one-family executioners, Jean-Baptiste being only seven years old. In fact had Anne-Marthe, his mother, died first, his grandmother Jeanne-Renee, a woman less committed to maintaining the family's vocation, could well have used his tender years as a reason to break the link. But Anne-Marthe was still alive, still the dominant spirit of the Sansons, still very much the matriarch. Within her burned a fierce flame of pride, a determination that the Sansons would never relinquish their honourable place in society, that of being the veritable keystone of law and order in the nation's capital. And suspecting that, despite the legal document, the authorities might conceivably appoint someone else of a more mature age, she visited the public prosecutor and ensured that her son's claim to the position was duly recorded.

In the same way as a caring mother gradually teaches her child the way of life a little at a time, here a toy, there a jigsaw puzzle, perhaps a bicycle, so Anne-Marthe introduced Jean-Baptiste to his future by degrees, taking him to the scaffold, there to watch a felon being branded, a woman being pilloried, a man being hanged or decapitated. And by 1737, when he was eighteen, she watched proudly as he performed his first execution as Monsieur de Paris.

However, far from exulting in his new vocation, Jean-Baptiste was repelled by it. An impressionable man, he was too aware of the inevitably pitiful state of his victims to remain unaffected, and after performing an execution he would ride out into the countryside, as if trying to outdistance his tormented emotions. Occasionally he visited one of his late father's friends, Jules Tronson, whose daughter Madeleine had been a playmate of his since childhood days. Now nineteen years of age, though old beyond his years, the idea of having a wife and family appealed strongly to him, and so in 1738 he asked Jules for his daughter's hand in marriage, consent gladly being given. His choice was well made, for Jules Tronson was a *questionaire* and Madeleine was therefore no stranger to the constraints and restrictions which surrounded those employed in administering justice.

As was the custom, a celebration was held on the evening prior to the marriage service, and despite the wet weather, the guests, waited on by the executioner's assistants appropriately clad, were enjoying themselves. As they danced to the music provided by a small orchestra one of the servants informed Jean-Baptiste that three strangers were at the door seeking shelter, having lost their way in the storm.

Hospitable as ever, the groom-to-be invited them in to join the festivities. The men were obviously of noble birth, one of them being resplendent in the uniform of a lieutenant in the Royal Irish Guards, the regiment of the Comte de Dillon, and he introduced himself as the Comte Thomas Arthur de Lally-Tollendal. All three joined in the celebrations, and it was not until the time came for them to continue on their way that one of them asked the name of their host. Their reactions on being informed that he was none other than the public executioner for the Paris region can well be imagined! But being young, and having imbibed enough to discard their inhibitions, they then asked whether they might inspect his 'tools of the trade'. Jean-Baptiste agreed and, leading them to the storeroom, showed them the branding irons, clubs and axes. Lally-Tollendal was particularly interested in the double-handed execution sword, with the word 'Justicia' engraved on its blade. Trying its edge for sharpness with his finger, he commented that no doubt only one blow from such a weapon would be necessary to remove a man's head. And when Jean-Baptiste concurred, the lieutenant exclaimed jocularly, 'Should I ever find myself in such a situation, I shall hold you to your promise!'

The young officer became a good friend of the family,

visiting them during his periods of leave in the capital. The Sansons felt proud at their friend's military achievements, for such was his prowess in battle that eventually he was promoted to Lieutenant-General and, in 1757, was posted to India as 'Commander of the French Settlements in Asia', with a force of four thousand soldiers with which to confront the English armies. And such were his rising fortunes that neither he nor Jean-Baptiste ever dreamed that the situation they had joked about on the wedding eve could ever arise, or that his friend the executioner would need to honour his promise.

Jean-Baptiste, despite his wife's support in a way of life which he had forced himself to accept as inevitable, became morose and gloomy, and his responsibilities on the scaffold brought him to a state of mind which even his regular attendances at Low Mass in the church of St Laurent failed to dispel.

At home however he settled down, happy in his new-found domesticity. His wife Madeleine bore him two children, first a daughter, Madeleine Claude Gabrielle, born about 1738, who would grow up to marry 'within the clan', namely Pierre Herrison, executioner of Melun, and then, on 15 February 1739, Charles-Henri was born, a boy destined to make his mark in the scrolls of history as 'Charles Le Grand', France's greatest executioner.

Shortly after the birth of their son, Jean-Baptiste's already despondent temperament received a further blow when his wife Madeleine died. Desperately needing a companion to sustain him and care for his children, after a decent period he married again, this time to Jeanne-Gabrielle Berger. That young lady came from a family of executioners who operated in the province of Touraine, and so marriage to Monsieur de Paris held no fears for her.

Their union was blessed with no fewer than eight children. First came Louis Charles Martin, born in 1744, a son who on growing up would learn his trade with Charles Le Grand and then become executioner of Tours in 1793, Dijon in 1807, and later in Auxerre. In turn he would also found a minor branch of headsmen by marrying Marie-Victoire de Charmoy, sister of the executioner of Amiens, and their son Louis Victor would be lord of the scaffold in Montpellier and, in 1806, in Genoa. When Italy ceased to belong to France, Louis Victor moved to Aix in 1814, and later lived with his mother in Paris.

A year later another boy was born to Jeanne-Gabrielle, and was christened after his uncle, Nicolas Charles Gabriel. He too followed the family tradition, becoming executioner of Blois, then at Montpellier, though he was dismissed for drunkenness in September 1800, dying in the same year.

Louis Cyr Charlemagne came next, born in 1748, and subsequently obtained the position of executioner of Provins in 1788. He married, first, Marie Madeleine Genevieve Herrison, who bore him three children, all of whom regrettably died in infancy. His second wife, Marie Fare Marguerite Gendron, born in Provins in 1759, gave her husband a son, Louis Henri Gabriel, in 1791. His father later became executioner at Versailles, where he died; he was not however succeeded by his son, for Louis Henri Gabriel, in a forlorn attempt to escape his terrible heredity, decided to become a locksmith, and so learned the trade at the town of Troyes. But destiny proved too powerful for him; shunned by the public, he gave up the profession and lived with his mother in Provins. Marrying, he had three children, a girl born in 1816, and two boys, born in 1815 and 1819 respectively. With no wage earner, the entire family was almost destitute, surviving only on the pension received by his mother as the widow of an executioner. In the National Archives, a letter by the prefect of Seine-et-Marne, dated 1823, describes their plight. Praising Louis Henri Gabriel, he wrote; 'He is a good locksmith though he has given up the attempt to find work. The profession practised by the father isolates this family from all kinds of society and, though they behave irreproachably, they live in a state of the greatest poverty and neglect.' Louis Henri Gabriel died in 1874 at the age of eighty-one.

In 1751 a daughter, Marie-Josephe, added a more feminine aspect to the male-dominated household. In her late teens she married a cousin, Jean-Louis Sanson, executioner of Reims, and had a daughter who, in 1819, worked in the linen trade in Paris.

Of the other four children, Pierre (1753), Jean-Baptiste Pierre born the following year, Joseph-Claude, who lived from 1757 to 1779, and lastly Gabrielle, at least two of the boys fell in with their father's wishes. One operated at Tours, perhaps with Louis Charles Martin; the other became a *questionaire*, an official torturer, in Paris, from 1 December 1779 to 16 October 1792. What became of the other two is not known, and so by virtue of that fact, perchance in some way they managed to elude the call of the scaffold.

In those days, when large families were the norm, the Sanson brood posed few problems. They were brought up strictly by their parents and attended church service every Sunday. Jean-Baptiste, when not required to execute the orders of the court, gave rein to the humane side of his nature by practising those medical skills inherited from his father and grandfather, and gained a reputation among his many patients, both rich and poor, for his expertise in mending broken bones and his ability to alleviate and cure minor ailments with his medicines and herbal remedies.

As usual, much difficulty arose over the education of the children, the very mention of the name of Sanson bringing instant rejection by school authorities. In an attempt to circumvent such reactions, the eldest son, Charles-Henri, was sent to a school in Rouen, in the vain hope that the implications of his family name would not be realized, that he might have the chance to be just another little French schoolboy learning his lessons. But it was not to be. Horror at his family's occupation outweighed all academic principles, and Jean-Baptiste was requested to remove the boy forthwith. And so Charles-Henri received private tuition from Abbé Grisel, a cleric who reportedly found the boy bright and intelligent, 'though somewhat weak at spelling'.

It was in 1750 that Jean-Baptiste decided, in the same way as he himself had been indoctrinated, to introduce his son to life – and death – on the scaffold, so that he too could assume the bloodstained mantle when required to do so. Forty-two more years would elapse before the advent of the guillotine, the device which would herald an era of quicker, if not more merciful death. Until that time many other methods of execution were at the disposal of the courts, including hanging, burning, decapitation by the sword and being drawn and quartered. Whichever method was first witnessed by young Charles-Henri, it must have been a half-curious, half-frightened 11-year-old boy who accompanied his father up the steps of the scaffold to watch an execution.

Nor was that initial experience an isolated one, for during those formative years Charles-Henri continued to take his place on the platform, deafened by the gloating cries of the frenzied mob, sickened by the spectacle of the noosed and suffocating victim or the decapitated corpse, as his father operated the gallows or deftly swung the sword.

Perhaps Jean-Baptiste had a premonition that his son would need to absorb as much as possible about the art of execution, for there is little doubt that the strain told on the older man. So much so, that in 1754, at the age of thirty-five, he suffered a severe stroke which, although not affecting his speech, paralysed his right side, thereby making it impossible to manipulate sword, noose or iron bar. Jeanne-Gabrielle consulted specialists, but upon being told that a cure was not possible, she and her husband retired to a small farmhouse in Brie-Comte-Robert, in the hopes that, without the malign influence of the scaffold, the recuperative effects of the countryside could bring about a recovery. And indeed it did, for in 1761 Jean-Baptiste applied for, and obtained, the post of executioner for the district in which they lived. However, he returned to the Paris scaffold just once more, some time later, there to assist his son Charles-Henri in a particularly poignant and horrific execution.

4   Charles-Henri: The Early Days

When Jean-Baptiste retired to Brie-Comte-Robert in 1754, his departure generated a rush of applications from those who wanted to obtain the lucrative post of Monsieur de Paris. They were hopeful too, for how could the 'traditional' Sanson successor, a mere boy of fifteen years of age, be considered qualified and capable? However they had reckoned without the family matriarch, Charles-Henri's redoubtable grandmother Anne-Marthe Dubut, who was fiercely determined that the Sanson tradition should be upheld at all costs. Accordingly, she took her grandson to the office of the public prosecutor and, brooking no arguments from other would-be executioners, established her grandson's claim to the succession, reinforcing this by paying the considerable sum of money required by the Treasury in respect of such official appointments. Charles-Henri, then, was duly authorized by Parliament to be deputy public executioner, though he would not be fully invested until his father's death.

Too young to swing the sword, not strong enough to wield the bone-crushing iron bar, nevertheless he was required, in his official capacity, to be in attendance on the scaffold while his more experienced assistants dealt out the punishment ordained by the courts. His first ordeal was not long in coming, for in January 1755 a criminal named Ruxton had been sentenced to be broken on the wheel. Accordingly the teenager was present as the victim had his limbs fractured one by one and then was finally put to death by a blow to the chest.

Charles-Henri was given little respite, for only three days elapsed before his next call to duty. Again the fearsome wheel was the instrument of retribution, and as the snow

swirled around the scaffold the young man forced himself to watch as the blows from the iron bar shattered the victim's arms and legs, crushing bone and sinew into pulp, and brutally reducing what had been a human being into a limp and helpless puppet. The criminal this time was a man called Mongeot, found guilty of murdering the husband of his mistress, Mme Lescombat. She too had been sentenced to death for inciting her lover but, having claimed to be pregnant, an interval of two months was permitted for verification, during which time she was held in prison. In March, her claim disproved, she joined the young executioner and his assistants on the scaffold. There, before a vast crowd of jeering spectators, she was hanged, so becoming the first woman to be executed in that fashion in Charles-Henri's term of office.

Duties such as this, together with presiding over his assistants as felons were whipped, branded or subjected to the pillory, helped somewhat to harden the fledgeling executioner, but could hardly have prepared him for what was to come when, on 5 January 1757, Robert-François Damiens tried to assassinate King Louis XV by stabbing him with a knife. The blade was deflected due to the fact that, because of the inclement weather, His Majesty wore two fur coats. But the royal survival did not excuse the heinous crime of attempted regicide, and accordingly the horrific judgement was read out by Parliament:

The Court declares Robert-François Damiens duly convicted of the crime of *lèse-majesté*, divine and human, for the very wicked, very abominable and very detestable parricide perpetrated on the King's person; and therefore condemns the said Damiens to *amende honorable* before the principal church of Paris, whither he shall be taken in a cart wearing only a shirt and holding a taper of the weight of two pounds; and then, on his knees, he shall say and declare that, wickedly and with premeditation, he has perpetrated the said very wicked, very abominable and very detestable parricide, and wounded the King with a knife in the right side, for which he repents and begs pardon of God, the King and Justice; and further the court orders that he then be taken to the Grève and, on a scaffold erected for the purpose, that his chest, arms, thighs and calves be burnt with pincers; his right hand, holding the knife with which he committed the said parricide, burnt in sulfur; that boiling oil, melted lead, and rosin and wax mixed with sulfur be poured into his wounds; and after that his body be pulled and dismembered by four horses, and the members and body consumed in fire, and the ashes scattered to the winds. The court orders that his property be confiscated to the King's profit; that before the said execution Damiens be subjected to the *question ordinaire et extraordinaire* to make him confess the names of his accomplices. Orders that the house in which he was born

be demolished, and that no other building be erected on that
spot. Decreed by Parlement 26 March 1757.

Such an unbelievably brutal sentence had not been passed
since that meted out to Ravaillac, the assassin of Henry IV
in 1610, and that it should fall to the lot of Charles-Henri to
administer filled the 18-year-old youth with horror. His
doughty grandmother, Anne-Marthe Dubut, came to his aid
and, bringing all her autocratic influence to bear, arranged
that, while Charles-Henri would need to be present in order
to regularize the proceedings, her other son, Nicolas
Gabriel, should perform the actual execution, with his
nephew's assistance.

Despite his own years in office, Nicolas Gabriel was also
overwhelmed by the enormity of the task; indeed he was so
appalled that he even considered resigning rather than
administer the sentence.

However he withdrew his resignation when, fortuitously,
a man named Soubise was located, whose grandfather had
actually meted out similar agonies to Ravaillac. Soubise,
himself a former official torturer, not only supplied details of
the designated punishment but, much to the Sansons' relief,
also offered to administer much of it personally, if
adequately rewarded.

Perforce, preparations went ahead. Four young, strong
horses were hired and the scaffold was erected in the square,
the Place de Grève. As the horses required sufficient space
in which to dismember the would-be assassin, a considerable
area was cleared, cordoned off with thick wooden palings
and heavily guarded by soldiers. This was necessary to
control the crowds for, as a Paris newspaper was to report,
'Every rooftop in the vicinity was covered with people, and
among the crowds which packed the square one could not
help but remark on how many women were present, women
of distinction. They seemed to weather the horrors of the
execution even better than the men, which fact does not
exactly do them honour.'

Meanwhile the two Sansons, Nicolas Gabriel and
Charles-Henri, wearing their traditional uniforms of blue
breeches and red jackets embroidered in black with the
symbols of their trade, the gibbet and the ladder, their attire

completed by pink, two-cornered hats, with the requisite swords at their waists, proceeded to the Conciergerie, the prison in which Damiens was held. There the victim, enveloped in a large leather bag from which only his head protruded, was carried in, accompanied by a priest. After sentence had been read out to him, he was taken into the adjoining torture chamber for interrogation by the judges, it being vital that the identities of any accomplices be ascertained.

One method employed was that of the 'boots', high leather boots reaching to the knee, the cords of which were gradually tightened until the intense pain brought screams of agony from Damiens. Within minutes he had fainted and had to be revived with sips of wine which were administered by Charles-Henri, the young executioner's innate sense of pity for his victims already becoming apparent.

The torture continued for two and a quarter hours, and included that of *estrapade*; Damiens' wrists being tied behind him, he was then hoisted from the ground, dislocating his shoulder-blades. No information being elicited, he was eventually lifted down and carried to the waiting tumbril by Charles-Henri and his assistants.

Meanwhile Nicolas Gabriel, on arriving at the scaffold, found things going badly wrong. Not only had the torturer Soubise, charged with procuring the lead, sulphur, wax and rosin, done nothing of the sort, he was, in fact, hopelessly drunk. Nor was that all, for the wood needed for the fire on which the ingredients would be heated was too damp to ignite. A scene of complete chaos prevailed among the leather-aproned assistants, quelled only by the arrival of the criminal lieutenant who, by issuing threats of dire retribution, managed to restore some form of order. Local shopkeepers, reluctant to supply the necessary materials for such a horrific purpose, were coerced into co-operating; meanwhile the tumbril had arrived, the victim, released from his leather confinement, having to sit on the scaffold steps and wait until all was ready.

At last the chafing dish, in which the sulphur was being burnt with hot coals, filled the atmosphere with acrid fumes, and Damiens was helped up on to the platform. There his right arm was tied to an iron bar so that the wrist extended

beyond the edge of the boards; Nicolas Gabriel brought the chafing dish and with trembling hands, started to sear Damiens's flesh with the blue flames. After three minutes the executioner desisted, unable to continue with the punishment as the victim screamed and writhed in agony. On seeing this, Charles-Henri detailed an assistant, André Legris, to take over, with the promise of an extra bonus.

The next stage was the application of the red-hot pincers, and this was administered as decreed by the sentence, Damiens's chest and limbs being nipped and burnt with the pincers, molten lead and pitch, rosin and liquid wax then being poured into the open wounds.

The semi-conscious victim was next carried down the steps and laid on the ground. Ropes secured about his ankles and wrists were tied to the harness of the four horses, the animals being spurred into action with shouts and whips. Unfortunately they were young horses and pulled without any co-ordination; this, coupled with the natural resistance of their victim's sinews and muscles, failed to bring the desired result, that of tearing his limbs off. Time was passing, the crowds were getting more and more agitated, until at last Charles-Henri sought consent from the judges present to sever the sinews in Damiens's armpits and groin with a knife and so bring merciful death to the suffering, still conscious victim. Approval was given, and within seconds Damiens's arms and legs were separated from his torso, the hideously mutilated creature dying almost immediately. Once the horses had been reined in, the blood-soaked, lacerated remains were gathered up and thrown on the roaring fire, the ashes, as decreed, then being dispersed to the four winds.

The horrific sight was witnessed by the Italian, Casanova, who wrote in his *Mémoires*, 'I watched the dreadful scene for four hours but was several times obliged to turn my face away and to close my ears as I heard his piercing shrieks, half his body having been torn away from him.'

In the months that followed, Charles-Henri developed into manhood. Musically talented, he played both the violin and cello, his favourite composer being Gluck, and he admitted that he found playing his instruments a solace after particularly trying executions. He would entertain his many

relatives at family parties, reunions in which his father and
stepmother would be brought from Brie-Comte-Robert,
Jean-Baptiste in his wheelchair, while grandmother Anne-
Marthe presided over the gathering as she sat embroidering
in her armchair.

Now as much a family tradition as the scaffold itself,
Charles-Henri studied anatomy, and supplied medical
schools with those corpses not claimed by their relatives. He
also treated the ailments of members of the poorer classes of
society who lived in his neighbourhood, and it was rumoured
that from the fat of his victims – *graisse de pendu* – he would
sometimes distil a cure for rheumatism (this source of
curative tissue was based on superstition and was widely
used in Europe during that and earlier centuries).

No portraits have survived the centuries, but contemporaries describe him as a man with classic features and a
pleasant manner. Ever mindful of his honoured ancestor, he
used the title 'Chevalier de Longval' and adopted a coat of
arms which incorporated a cracked bell, a play on the words
sans son, without sound.

He adopted the habits of an elegant Parisian gentleman,
and took to wearing tailored coats of blue cloth, apparel
which brought down on his head the disapproval of the
public prosecutor, who pointed out that that particular
colour was the privilege of the aristocracy, matching the
alleged colour of their blood – and Sanson was not of that
social class. Defeated but defiant, the young man
re-equipped his wardrobe with green suits, the jackets being
cut away in a distinctive style, and this fashion caught on
among the French dandies, who deemed it 'à la mode' to be
seen wearing 'Sanson Green'.

Open-air sports also appealed to Charles-Henri, in
particular that of hunting, and it was while returning from a
day's shooting that an event occurred which demonstrated
the pride he felt in his profession, despite all its concomitant
horrors. Better than any impersonal account are the actual
words by the subject himself, and in this respect I am
fortunate to be able to quote from Charles-Henri's own
extensive diaries, entries which reveal the principles guiding
him, and the way in which he viewed his own way of life.

After a long day's shooting [he wrote] I was entering an inn at dinner time and found myself in the company of Mme la Marquise de X—, who was returning from her country house to Paris. This lady bowed, offered me a seat and, after half an hour's conversation, she at length asked me what my profession was. Of course I replied that I was an officer of Parliament. She immediately requested that our dinners should be served together, and we made such a gay and pleasant repast that on both sides it seemed as if the heart had something to do with our conversation. After dessert I ordered my horses and postchaise and retired, but hardly had I left the room when a gentleman who was acquainted with the marquise came up and asked her, 'Madame, do you know the young man who has just dined with you?' 'No,' she answered, 'he told me he was an officer of Parliament.' 'He is the executioner of Paris; I know him quite well. He has just executed a man, or rather, superintended an execution, for he seldom does the work himself.'

At these words the Marquise nearly fainted. She remained speechless with confusion, shed tears and, remembering that I had touched her hand, she asked for a basin of water, and washed her hands. She stepped into her carriage and during the journey bethought herself of the means of avenging herself. Shortly after her arrival in Paris she presented a petition to Parliament in which, after relating what had taken place, she asked that I should be sentenced to beg her pardon, with a rope round my neck, for the insult of which she said I had been guilty, and that for the safety of the public, I should henceforth have to wear a distinctive sign so that all should know me.

In his spirited defence before the court, Charles-Henri pointed out that if HE were guilty of carrying out ignoble acts, that is, executions, those trying him now were equally guilty, because they who ordered him to commit that 'crime' of execution were more guilty than he who committed it.

Moreover [Sanson continued] I am quite aware that all public offices are not equally honourable; they are creditable only because they are useful to society; but according to the latter principle, mine stands in the first rank. What would the

State do if it were suppressed for a single day? The whole kingdom would be a vast field of brigandage; the most sacred laws would be trodden under foot, virtue would be despised and vice would prevail. There would be no other law than the law of the strongest; murder, rapine and theft would be fearlessly committed under the very eyes of Justice. It would be useless to punish and condemn; pecuniary penalties do not frighten penniless brigands; sentences entailing physical penalties would be laughed at if there was no one to carry them out; for I venture to say, gentlemen, they do not fear your sentences; it is my beheading sword which makes them tremble; it is in the shadow of that sword that innocence breathes freely, that the police are powerful and that public order has prevailed.

The God of armies has placed the sword in the hands of the King to punish crime and protect innocence. Being unwilling to wield it himself, he has done me the honour to entrust it to my hands. I am the guardian of this treasure, which is the distinctive symbol of his sovereignty. It is not to you that he has given it in trust; the culprit deserves punishment because of his crime, not of your sentence; it is the law which inflicts punishment; I, as public minister, use the weapon with which I have been entrusted. I punish crime and avenge outraged virtue; this gives my employment a pre-eminence and a degree of elevation which brings it in closer connection with the throne.

I know that my office is considered dishonourable because I slay men; hence the feeling of horror with which I am regarded. This is the result of mere prejudice, which would be quickly dispelled if the facts were examined without prejudice. Witness the profession of arms, which is highly esteemed, although it has for its object to shed the blood of the enemy. Ask a soldier what his profession is and he will tell you that, like me, he is a slayer of men. Yet his company is never shunned, and no one thinks he is disgraced by eating in his company. I only kill culprits, and a man who has done his duty has nothing to fear from me. I merely purge society of the monsters who disturb its repose, and scarcely a week passes without there being occasion for me to punish crime and avenge the rights of innocence.

It will not be denied, I suppose, that I am a member of

Parliament and perhaps, I may say, one of its most useful members. I have the honour to be the fourth of my family to whom it has descended from father to son, and if hereditary nobility were attached to it, as it ought to be, I might stand on even ground with Mme la Marquise. Innate feeling honours the soldier who slays, absolves the duellist who slays, but brands the executioner; but how can it condemn him without also discarding capital punishment?

These eloquent and telling words, perhaps even relevant to this century, won the day, and no more was heard of the lady's protest.

A close friend of Charles-Henri was Abbé Gomart, a priest whose religious duties were to accompany those doomed to die. He would mop the brow of one being broken on the wheel, bring spiritual comfort to those being hanged. It was a daunting task and one in which he occasionally needed Charles-Henri's support and hospitality. Whilst dining at the Sanson residence one day, he expressed his fears regarding a young lady he described as his niece, although in actual fact he was her father, her mother being a dressmaker. Her name was Marie Jeanne de Vaubernier, and her morals, he said sadly, were causing him increasing concern. Convent educated, she had left to become apprenticed to a famous costumier on the rue St Honoré in Paris and whilst engaged there had become acquainted with the elegant ladies of the court, their somewhat wayward and daring lifestyle encouraging her to act likewise. Ravishingly beautiful, the abbé explained, she had begun to lead a life of sin and dissipation.

At that, Charles-Henri promised to help his old friend and so made the acquaintance of Marie Jeanne de Vaubernier, agreeing at once that the young lady was indeed overwhelmingly alluring. Despite having no motive in mind other than to help her mend her ways, he was nevertheless deeply attracted to her; his attentions, however, were not reciprocated, for the lady was aiming far higher than a liaison with the public executioner.

They parted, and she soon ingratiated her way into fashionable society where, known as Mademoiselle Lange, she won the attention of Louis XV who, in order to elevate her status and facilitate her entry into court circles, arranged that she marry the Comte Guillaume du Barry. And it was as Jeanne Bécu Gommard de Vaubernier, Comtesse du Barry, that she achieved what was undoubtedly her life's ambition, that of being a monarch's mistress. Fate would once more bring Charles-Henri and Jeanne together, but not for another twenty-seven years, when he would have the unenviable task of guillotining the woman to whom he had been so much attracted.

A more enduring love, however, entered his life when he reached the age of twenty-six. On his hunting trips he would frequently stop at the house of M. Jugier, a market gardener, and there partake of a glass of wine and refreshments while engaging in congenial conversation with his host. The eldest daughter of the family was Marie-Anne, with whom, after many visits, he fell in love. Traditionally he should have married into another family of executioners but, mindful of his antecedents as a chevalier, he snobbishly felt that such a union would be beneath him; accordingly he proposed to Marie-Anne, and was accepted.

His fiancée, six years older than he, was a warm-hearted and caring woman and, in the event, proved to be a devoted wife to one who, had they but known it, would have to face the horrors of the French Revolution and the harvest of death it brought to his scaffold.

They were married on 20 January 1765, the wedding taking place in the church of Saint Pierre Montmartre, and Marie-Anne soon established a comfortable and well-conducted household, thereby lightening her husband's tasks as he administered the penalties of the law to the wrong-doers of Paris.

It was on 9 May 1766 that a figure from the past re-entered his life, none other than the young officer who had joined the festivities at his father's wedding celebrations twenty-eight years earlier – the Comte de Lally-Tollendal. Since that time the soldier's military career had exceeded all expectations; in 1740 he obtained command of a regiment which took his name, and at the age of thirty-seven was promoted to the rank of lieutenant-general.

When war was declared between France and England in 1756, his leadership on the field of battle was invaluable. Of

Irish descent and a fervent supporter of the exiled Stuarts, he devised a plan to land 10,000 French troops on the English coast to support the claims of the Pretender, but this proved impracticable. Instead he was given the command of a French expeditionary force in India, and there achieved many initial successes. But his violent temper and his contempt for all action other than brute force led him into making mistakes, errors which were to prove disastrous. He allowed his troops to ransack captured towns, and permitted the violation of Hindu sanctuaries, resulting in the desertion of the native forces who previously supported the French. Obstinate and cruel, he even sentenced natives suspected of spying to be blown from cannon.

Defeat followed defeat, and eventually he was led into a trap, his troops being surrounded and besieged at Pondicherry. Forced to accept an unconditional surrender, he was sent to England as a prisoner, but on hearing that he was being blamed for losing India to the English, and of misappropriating public funds, he obtained parole from his captors and, as hot-headed as ever, returned to face his enemies in Paris.

At his trial, in which he defended himself vehemently, he was accused of abuse of power, violence to his soldiers and the natives. Scapegoat or not for the loss of a colony of such inestimable value to the French, on 6 May 1766 he was sentenced to be decapitated by the sword.

On hearing the result of the trial, Charles-Henri's father Jean-Baptiste, recalling his first meeting with the comte nearly three decades earlier and the promise he had made, albeit jocularly, hastened to Paris and joined Charles-Henri and his old friend on the scaffold. In a work written by Henri-Clement Sanson, the last of the Sanson line, the author described the scene:

> Jean-Baptiste showed him his withered arm and pointing to his son who was standing at the other end of the scaffold so as to conceal the sight of the sword from the unfortunate Lally, he said that he was too old to strike, and that his promise must be discharged by a stronger arm and steadier hand than his. Lally thanked him by an inclination of the head and, as Charles-Henri approached, Lally requested that his hands,

secured behind his back, be freed. The executioner explained that it was impossible, it was the custom. 'Then help me take this vest off and give it to your father,' the comte said.

Charles-Henri obeyed and took off the vest, which was made of a valuable golden tissue of India. Each button was a large ruby of the finest water. After this Lally knelt and said, 'And now you can strike!'

Charles-Henri raised the weapon and let it fall on the old man's neck. But the hair, which had not been cut but only raised, deflected the blade, and the head did not fall. The blow was so violent that Lally was struck down to the earth, but he sprang to his feet in a moment, glaring at Jean-Baptiste Sanson with a lamentable expression of indignation and reproach.

At this sight the old executioner rushed towards his son and, suddenly recovering his strength, took the bloody sword from his hand, and before the cry of horror which rose from the crowd had subsided, Lally's head was rolling on the scaffold; the promise had been fulfilled.

Two months later Charles-Henri, no doubt chastened by his failure to deliver the sword blow accurately, was once again faced with the prospect of dealing death to a nobleman. This time it was the Chevalier de la Barre, who had been wrongly accused of sacrilege and sentenced to death. On meeting the executioner, the victim referred to Lally-Tollendal's ordeal, saying that he hoped he would not have to suffer as Lally had done, adding, 'I was always something of a dandy, and I cannot reconcile myself to the idea that my poor head, which they said was not altogether ugly, should horrify those who see it.'

Charles-Henri reassured him, and on the day of execution, 1 July 1766, he led the condemned man on to the scaffold. There he showed the sword to the chevalier, who remarked on its sharpness. The executioner then bade him kneel, but de la Barre refused, saying vehemently, 'I am no criminal; do your duty. I shall give you no trouble, only be quick.'

Raising the heavy sword, Sanson swung it, striking with such vigour and dexterity that it severed the spine and went through the neck without dislodging the head from the shoulders. For a few seconds the upright figure of the victim swayed – and true or not, witnesses say they heard Charles-Henri exclaim, 'Shake yourself – it's done!'

The Sansons had two children, both boys. Henri, born in 1767, eventually succeeded his father. The other, Gabriel, was born two years later and, as was to be expected, both assisted on the scaffold from an early age. Gabriel however never became an accredited executioner, losing his life in a particularly tragic accident in 1792.

Following the Lally-Tollendal débâcle, Jean-Baptiste's infirmity and general weakness began to tell on him. Bereft of his wife Jeanne-Gabrielle who had died some time earlier, his health failing fast, he formally resigned his post as the

Paris executioner on 30 July 1778. His daughter-in-law Marie-Anne nursed him devotedly during his decline and it was she who closed his eyes when he finally passed away a month later, and broke the sad news to Charles-Henri when he returned from superintending an execution.

Members of the Sanson family gathered for the funeral in the church of St Laurent, the coffin being interred in the family vault. Shortly afterwards Charles-Henri duly received his *lettre de provision*, the document which appointed him to the post of Executioner of the High Works, for which he paid a sum of six thousand livres to the Treasury, and would henceforth be known as Monsieur de Paris.

But there were, of course, other nicknames, few being altogether complimentary. One was that of *bourreau*, an epithet particularly disliked by Charles-Henri. Although the word could mean 'hangman', it was used in the context of 'brute' or 'bully'. The executioner consulted a magistrate, who informed him that a likely origin was the word *bourrea*, Latin for the willow switch with which the lictors of ancient Rome punished adulterers. Another possible derivation was one originating from 1260, taken from a priest called Borel who obtained the fief of Bellemcombre on condition that he should hang the thieves of the district. As he was a priest, and as the Church mentioned in its prayers that it did not approve of the spilling of blood, he paid a layman to discharge his functions. Despite this, it became the custom to call Richard Borel 'le Borel', and to describe as 'Boreaux' all those who put criminals to death. The orthography of the name was altered and became 'bourreau' or 'bourreaux'. Although not intended to be derogatory, it bore a contemptuous significance even in the sixteenth century.

Incensed by the disparaging label, Charles-Henri appealed to Louis XVI to forbid the word being applied to him, and a prohibition was accordingly issued on 12 January 1787, a decree rarely complied with by the public or the Press.

Other nicknames were 'The People's Avenger' and 'Executioner of the Criminal Sentences'; another was 'Charlot', because of his Christian name, and also *Sans Farine*, a play on words, since executioners used bran sacks, *sacs de son*, as containers for the heads they had severed. The sacks would be without bran, hence 'San son', without grain. And when the guillotine held sway, the name 'Admiral of the Red Theatre' was bestowed on Charles-Henri, reflecting his starring role on the 'stage', the boards of the bloody scaffold.

Such was the multiplicity of crimes which carried corporal or capital punishment, that hardly a day passed without Sanson's services being required. One unusual case involved a lady of society, one Jeanne de Saint-Remy Valois, wife of the Comte de la Motte. A witty, attractive and elegant woman, she had become acquainted with Cardinal de Rohan, a powerful man at Court, and managed to persuade the prelate that she was a close friend of the Queen's.

Her ingenious scheme revolved about a magnificent necklace made by the crown jewellers, MM. Boemer and Bossange, on behalf of Louis XV for his mistress Mme du Barry. The King had died before it could be completed, and du Barry had been exiled to England. The necklace, which consisted of 541 precious stones, was offered to the new king, but its price, 1,800,000 livres, was considered too high, and the jewellers promised to make a rich present to whoever could find a buyer.

Comtesse de la Motte wove her plot, telling the cardinal that the Queen wanted to buy the necklace with her own money, without the King's knowledge, and so desired the cardinal to purchase it on her behalf. And she handed over an authorization forged by a man named Marc-Antoine Retaux de Villette, purporting to be from the Queen, to be given to the jewellers, pledging payment.

Accordingly the necklace was given to the cardinal, who in turn passed it to Comtesse de la Motte for delivery to the Queen. Except that it never reached the royal palace; instead Jeanne de la Motte sold some of the gems, her husband taking the rest to England, where he promptly disposed of 300 gems for £14,000, a veritable fortune in those days.

The jewellers, having received no payment, complained to the palace, and inquiries were instituted, with the result that all involved, including Jeanne, the forger Villette and the cardinal, were put on trial. The latter dignitary was cleared of all charges, Villette was sentenced to be banished from the kingdom, and others in the plot were suitably punished.

Jeanne de la Motte herself was found guilty, the sentence being that she should be whipped, branded on both shoulders with the letter 'V' (*voleuse*, thief), and imprisoned for life. On hearing this, Charles-Henri sought clarification of that part of the sentence which stipulated that the prisoner should be 'beaten and birched naked'; the ambiguous reply he was given was that he was to arrange the affair to take place as discreetly as possible, and to temper the severity of the sentence with humanity. Not that the condemned woman was aware of the sentence, for as was the judicial custom, the horrific details would not be divulged to her until the actual day on which they were to be administered.

Villette the forger was the first to be dealt with; in accordance with the ritual of banishment

> he was brought from the prison by the executioner, with a halter about his neck, to one of the gates of the city, where his sentence was read out; after which, a loaf of bread was presented to him by the executioner who then pointed out his way to the country and, with great solemnity, turned the culprit's back upon Paris, gave him a smart kick on the breeches, and bade him never to return!

It was then Jeanne's turn to receive drastic punishment. On 21 June 1786 Charles-Henri was sent for and informed that the prisoner had shown great displays of temper whilst in prison, and would no doubt do so again when informed of her sentence. Aware of his responsibilities and also that, the Comtesse being of noble blood, he would have to administer the beating himself rather than delegate it to an underling as he usually did, he realized that he would have to take all measures necessary to minimize any disturbance.

He began by obtaining information about the woman's habits, and heard that she was on very friendly terms with the gaoler's wife, who attended her in prison. Following the executioner's instructions this woman entered the prisoner's cell and told her she was wanted in the corridor. Comtesse de la Motte was in bed; she turned her face towards the wall and said that she was sleepy and could not get up so early. The gaoler's wife then said that it was her counsel who wished to see her, and so the prisoner jumped out of bed and got dressed.

As she was leaving the room, one of the executioner's assistants, who was behind the door, seized her arm and thrust it under his, his colleague doing the same with her other arm, but Comtesse de la Motte, displaying such strength as could hardly have been expected from a woman, shook away their grasp and retreated towards the door. Charles-Henri, however, had positioned himself in front of it, and the woman stopped and looked at him.

> She was [wrote Charles-Henri later] rather small in stature, but extremely well made. Her countenance was sufficiently pleasant to conceal for a time the irregularity of her features, although they were full of charm; and it was only after minute examination that one discovered that her nose was very sharp, that her expressive mouth was large, and that her eyes were somewhat small. What was remarkable was the thickness and length of her hair, the whiteness of her skin, and the smallness of her hands and feet. She wore a silk déshabillé, striped brown and white, and covered with small nosegays of roses, and her head was covered by an embroidered cap.

While she was eyeing Charles-Henri as if about to leap at him, the other assistants and four police officers surrounded her. She realized that resistance was useless when the executioner said, 'We wish you to listen to your judgement, madame.' The woman shuddered; she clenched her hands, looked down, then raised her head and led the way to the main hall where the clerk awaited them. At the first words which proclaimed her guilt, the strongest emotion appeared on Comtesse de la Motte's face. Her eyes rolled in their sockets; she bit her lip and the hitherto pretty face became a mask of fury.

Charles-Henri went on to say that he had foreseen trouble and was prepared. It was just as well, for as the clerk came to the penalties, the woman's rage burst out with extraordinary violence. She fell backwards so suddenly that her head would have been fractured on the stones had not the executioner caught her in his arms. It was impossible to finish the reading of the sentence. Jeanne's strength increased as the awareness of her fate flashed through her mind, and a protracted struggle ensued between her and those attempting to pinion her.

She was at length tied up and carried down to the courtyard. The scaffold had been erected opposite the gate, which had been left open. Despite the fact that it was only six o'clock in the morning, a crowd of hundreds had gathered, and as her bonds were loosened she ran towards the edge of the scaffold, a further struggle taking place as, with an effort, they managed to strip the clothing from her, and force her to lie face down on the bench so that Charles-Henri could administer the beating.

A vivid description of the scene was portrayed in a journal written by Nicolas Ruault:

> Her whole body was revealed – her superb body, so exquisitely proportioned. At the flash of those white thighs and breasts, the rabble broke the stunned silence with whistles, catcalls, and shouted obscenities. The prisoner slipping from his grasp, the executioner, branding iron in hand, had to follow her as she writhed and rolled across the paving stones of the courtyard to the very foot of the grand staircase.
>
> The delicate flesh sizzled under the red-hot iron. A light bluish vapour floated about her loosened hair. At that moment her entire body was seized with a convulsion so violent that the second letter 'V' was applied, not on her shoulder, but on her breast, her beautiful breast.
>
> Mme de la Motte's tortured body writhed in one last convulsive moment. Somehow she found strength enough to turn and sink her teeth into the executioner's shoulder, through the leather vest to the flesh, bringing blood. Then she fainted.

Charles-Henri, regretting the additional though unavoidable agony he had inflicted on the first victim he had ever personally branded, ordered the comtesse to be put in a coach and taken to the Saltpêtrière prison. Having recovered *en route*, she tried to throw herself under the wheels as she was alighting, and once in the cell she thrust the corner of a bedsheet into her throat in a frenzied attempt to choke herself.

Her imprisonment lasted, not for life, but for a brief ten months. With the aid of a bribed·sentry she escaped dressed as a man and got away to England. There she joined her husband in London, where she died in 1791.

Mention has been made earlier of the fearsome punishment whereby felons were broken on the wheel, the ancient French statutes listing no fewer than one hundred and fifty different crimes that carried this dire penalty. An edict issued during the reign of Francis I (1494–1547) directed that this punishment should be inflicted particularly on highwaymen and thieves, and such was the prevalence of that type of crime, it is hardly surprising that many of Charles-Henri's clients were executed in this manner. Among those listed in his diaries are André-Etienne Petit, for common theft; Jean Brouage, for stealing linen; Marie Picard and her 17-year-old son Pierre, for robbery and murder; Charlotte Beuton, for murder; Paul Darel, for theft, and many others.

Although Charles-Henri only supervised this horrendous method and, if authorized, administered the death-dealing, merciful retentum (the strangling cord or final blow to the chest) as early in the proceedings as he dared, there was no doubt that he abhorred its very existence in the penal code. And so although in retrospect he welcomed the 'Louschart Affair' as being instrumental in its abolition, at the time it seemed fraught with danger for himself and his assistants.

In August 1788 Mathurin Louschart, an elderly blacksmith, lived near Versailles, his housekeeper being a Madame Verdier. Mathurin's son Jean lived nearby, a young man whose republican tendencies conflicted violently with those of his royalist father. Many arguments on the subject took place, Mathurin being supported by Mme Verdier, a woman who was not only determined to end the romance blossoming between Jean and her daughter Helen, but who also intended to drive Jean out of the family altogether by persuading her employer to propose marriage to Helen; this would then leave the field clear for her to inherit her employer's estate.

To escape from such a situation the young couple decided to elope, and on the evening planned, Jean, arriving at his father's door, heard Helen scream. On rushing in he found Mme Verdier beating her daughter for her refusal to accept Mathurin's proposal of marriage.

The young man, intent on defending his sweetheart, immediately intervened, and in the furious row which followed Mathurin seized a hammer and threw it at his son. Fortunately it missed, and in the shocked silence that followed, Jean picked it up and turned to leave. As he did so, he threw the tool contemptuously back over his shoulder into the room, and strode out of the house. But quite unbeknown to him, the heavy hammer had struck his father, killing him instantly.

Jean was arrested and, overwhelmed with remorse, refused to put forward any defence at his trial; instead he accepted the verdict of guilty and the sentence that he was to be broken on the wheel, and stated that he was ready to die for his crime. But public feeling ran high at such an unjust verdict for what was manifestly a tragic accident, and when Charles-Henri arrived in the town to perform the execution, he immediately became aware of the rising tension. The carpenters constructing the scaffold were being harassed and impeded in their work, his assistants assaulted and jeered at, so when the scaffold was completed, he ordered a stout palisade to be erected around it to protect it from the vengeful inhabitants. And in order that the number of spectators be reduced to a minimum, the execution was arranged to take place at 4.30 in the morning.

Jean Louschart, resigned to his fate, was taken by cart to the market-place under a strong guard of police and soldiers. As they entered the square Charles-Henri felt mounting apprehension as he saw the vast crowds which had gathered, apprehension which turned to alarm when their prisoner, turning to call farewell to Helen standing by the roadside, was contradicted by a loud voice exclaiming, 'It is only *au revoir*, Jean; are good fellows like you to be broken on the wheel?'

On reaching the scaffold the executioner wasted no time, but even as he urged his unresisting victim up the steps, the mob broke through the barriers and rushed the scaffold.

One man seized Louschart and, untying his bonds, escorted him down into the jostling crowd, where he quickly disappeared from view. Charles-Henri's position was now desperately serious as the crowd advanced menacingly and surrounded him on the scaffold; separated from his assistants, he was without any means of defending himself. Just as he was giving himself up for lost, one of the ringleaders seized his arm and cried, 'Fear nothing, Charlot; we don't want to harm you, but your tools. From now on you must kill your customers without making them suffer.' And turning to the crowd he shouted, 'Let him pass, and take care he is not hurt.'

Hustled down the steps, the executioner withdrew to a safe distance and watched, partly aghast, partly elated, as the villagers not only smashed the dreaded wheel into fragments, but also demolished the scaffold, throwing the pieces of timber into the very fire which had been kindled to consume Jean Louschart's mutilated remains.

After dispersing to their homes, the inhabitants braced themselves for the dire reprisals that were bound to be levied against them when news of the destruction they had wreaked reached the authorities in Paris. But when the account of the trial and the public's reactions was brought to the attention of the King, he not only pardoned Jean Louschart, but decreed that the penalty itself would be stricken from the statute books; no more would victims suffer the appallingly slow and agonizing death of being broken on the wheel, and perhaps no one was more overjoyed at the royal decision than Monsieur de Paris himself.

The abolition of the wheel was but one of the actions taken by the authorities at that time in an attempt to alleviate the unrest among the French populace, but all came far too late to restore public morale. Such were the harrowing living conditions endured by the lower classes, so widespread the poverty and destitution, that an eruption of violent civil unrest seemed only a matter of weeks away. Even Charles-Henri, his debts mounting, his salary from the Treasury long overdue, had to petition the King; for if the executioner was in a debtor's prison, who would perform the executions?

His plea resulted in an audience with Louis XVI in the royal palace, the meeting being described in the family memoirs:

The King was standing near a window which opened on to the park. Charles-Henri, intimidated by the presence of royalty, dared advance no further than the threshold, so that the few words they spoke were exchanged at some distance.

Louis wore a lilac coat embroidered with gold, short breeches and pumps; the blue and red ribbons of the Order of St Louis hung across his white satin waistcoat. A lace collar and frill was partly covered by a loose cravat which showed the prominent muscles of his neck. The King was of strong but common build. His hair was powdered and curled and tied back with a ribbon at the nape of his neck.

'You have sent in a claim for the sums that are due to you,' he said without turning round or looking at the executioner. 'I have ordered that your accounts be examined and settled without delay, but the State is poor for the present, and your claim is for 136,000 livres, I believe.'

'I thank your Majesty with as much gratitude as respect,' answered Charles-Henri. 'But I beseech your Majesty to remember that my debts have so considerably increased that my creditors will not wait any longer, and that they threaten my liberty.'

At these words the King turned round and cast a rapid glance at the executioner. 'Wait a moment,' he said. 'I must see to this directly.' Ringing a bell, he summoned an official and ordered, 'Fetch me a safe-conduct and enter these names on it.'

The document read:

His Majesty, being desirous of giving Monsieur Charles-Henri Sanson the means attending his occupation, has given him a safe-conduct for a period of three months, during which His Majesty orders his creditors to take no proceedings against him; to all solicitors, police officers, or others, not to arrest him or molest him in any way; and if, in spite of the said prohibition, he be imprisoned, His Majesty also orders that he be set free immediately. His Majesty also orders that the present safe-conduct be available only after it has been registered at the office of the Garde du Commerce.

Delivered at Versailles on the nineteenth of April seventeen hundred and eighty nine ... Louis.

Having duly signed it, the King handed it to Charles-Henri, who accepted it and respectfully bent his knee. And as he left the palace apartment the Queen, Marie Antoinette, and the King's sister Madame Elizabeth, passed him in the corridor; he had thus been in the presence, on the same day, of the three royal persons whose lives he was subsequently to end beneath the guillotine's blade.

Three months later, on 14 July 1789, the people rose against the authorities. Frenzied crowds surged through the streets, looting and burning property, seizing arms from the arsenals and gunshops. Needing gunpowder, and also to destroy the hated symbol of authority, they attacked the Bastille. This formidable fortress, built four centuries earlier to defend the capital from attack from the east, had eight drum towers, a moat and drawbridges. Used as a prison, it was guarded by 110 men and fifteen cannon, and even while negotiations for a peaceful surrender were in progress, the mob attacked, supported by the artillery of the French Guard and Militia. Withering return fire was directed by the defenders, who had set fire to haycarts as a smokescreen.

For two hours the battle raged, cannon balls causing havoc among the attackers, while the artillery's missiles battered the heavily defended doors. At last, such was the intensity of the onslaught, the fortress was eventually overrun, the mob streaming in to pillage and destroy. But little was achieved, only seven blind, crippled or unwilling inmates being released. Of the prisoners, one was an Irishman named Clotworthy Skeffington Massareen who, detained as a debtor, occupied not a cell, but a comfortable apartment on the first floor!

The conditions in the ancient gaol were deplorable, it being later reported that the dungeons, foul and noxious, were infested with rats, lizards and toads. In an angle of each cell was a camp-bed consisting of planks resting on iron bars fixed to the dank walls. The dungeons were secured by double doors three inches thick, the inner surfaces covered by iron plates. Elsewhere were iron cages eight feet high by six feet wide, in one of which was found a man's skeleton.

The human cost of the battle was high. Ninety-eight of the attackers were killed and almost as many wounded. Of the defenders, eighty lost their lives, a further seventy being injured. The Governor of the Bastille, the Marquis de Launay, was captured and beheaded with a butcher's knife savagely wielded, it was said, by a cook named Desnot, but this was later denied by the owner of a Paris tavern, one Jourdan, who claimed the 'honour' himself. During a subsequent attack on the palace of Versailles, he decapitated three of the Household Guards, later joining a gang of robbers and terrorizing the district of Avignon.

When a general amnesty was declared, 'Jourdan the Head-Chopper' as he liked to be known, took advantage of its terms and by devious means achieved the almost unbelievable position of officer in charge of the local gendarmerie! Once in that influential capacity he extracted large sums of money from affluent business men by threatening to report them to the Tribunal. Nor did he stop at that. Any 'mam'selle' who took his fancy was at risk, unless her parents similarly made it worth his while.

However, retribution eventually caught up with him; in May 1794 reports of his extortionate activities reached the Committee of Public Safety in Paris and at his trial he was informed that he would be introduced to a REAL, professional head-chopper – Charles-Henri Sanson himself.

Having bought several bottles of wine from the gaoler before boarding the tumbril, Jourdan was almost drunk by the time the scaffold was reached, and the executioner's assistants had to half-carry him up the steps. Once there they wasted little time in strapping him to the bascule and, for once feeling no pity for his victim, Charles-Henri is reputed to have exclaimed, 'Here – sleep with your mistress!' as he released the blade.

On 26 August 1789 the 'Declaration of the Rights of Man' was proclaimed which, in effect, heralded the French Revolution, though not as yet its full cataclysmic intensity. The new brooms went into action; hundreds of street names commemorating royalty were changed to more plebeian ones, references to saints and religious events were banned,

as were the titles 'monsieur' and 'madame'. These were to
be replaced by 'citoyen' and 'citoyenne', for everyone,
royalty, aristocrats and commoners alike, were equal under
the new democratic regime.

Other radically sweeping changes were to take place
within the coming months, for with a stroke of a pen the
authorities swept into oblivion all feudal rights, manorial
courts of law, provostships, and ancient privileges.

As far as executioners were concerned, these measures
deprived them of what they considered to be their rightful
dues and, in many instances, the very wherewithal to carry
out their official functions. By 1790 the governing Assembly
responded to the profession's demands and complaints by
first asking Charles-Henri to state his own case.

Sanson, whose safe conduct from his creditors, signed by
the king in April 1789, had long since expired, was only too
willing to comply, and he penned a statement which was
historical in its own way, revealing as it does the business
and domestic necessities of an eighteenth-century executioner. (The 'livre' quoted was a unit of currency, being
worth 20 sous, 24 livres being 1 louis. It is estimated that an
income of 300 livres a year would provide reasonable living
for one person at that time. However, the costs listed are of
little relevance since the country's finances were in such a
parlous state that in 1789 the Treasury had been forced to
issue 'assignats', paper money backed by the value of the
estates confiscated from the Church and *émigrés*. This
currency in turn rapidly became worthless as a result of
over-issue and accelerating inflation.)

Charles-Henri's statement read:

Memorandum of information concerning the Executioner of
Criminal Judgements in the town of Paris.

In the earliest days the only allowance granted to the
Executioners of Criminal Judgements in the town of Paris
was a toll known as the right of havage, which they levied on
all kinds of provisions that were brought into the town to be
sold. This toll came to a considerable amount. It was always
levied until the month of September 1719, when it was
suppressed by letters patent.

The executioner, being left without resources, then

presented a statement of the position he was in, and was asked to draw up another, showing the expenses he was obliged to defray. The sum at that time amounted to 16,000 francs, and was granted to him by way of compensation for the right of havage, by an edict of 14 January 1727.

This provided for the payment of the executioner's expenses at a very moderate rate, which was arbitrary; but in 1767 the King, by an edict, made himself responsible for all executioners' expenses connected with offences committed against the seigneurial courts, provided that the royal judge received a statement of the claim within twenty-four hours. By this means all the courts of justice came under the control of the King, who paid very moderately.

This edict deprived the executioner of at least 20,000 livres a year. This enormous deficit was within an ace of reducing him to penury. On his making very urgent representations the evidence of his ruined condition led to the most minute inquiries being made. These inquiries were carried out under the orders of the Controller-General and the Intendant of Paris who, having convinced themselves of the justice of the executioner's request for an increase of pay, discussed the matter with M. de Beaumont, Intendant of Domains, and granted the executioner a larger sum for his professional expenses, regulating the amount on the scale that is still adopted.

Before the passing of the decree that suppressed the provostship and viscounty of Paris the executioner had in his ward six hundred jurisdictions, for which he was responsible, and for the service of which he required, and still requires, the sums specified below:

Expenses of the Executioner

Two of his brothers to whom he gives 600 livres each, to answer the magistrates and give orders to the servants when there are executions to be carried out at several places on the same day   1200
For four servants, 300 livres a year each   1200
For three carters, 300 livres a year each   900
For one cook per year   200

For four horses, for use in town and country	2000
The building of three carriages and a tumbril	300
Harness and upkeep of horses	150
The farrier, 50 livres for each horse per year	200
For the executioner's mother, a pension ordained from the earliest time by decree of the court	1200
For the food of sixteen persons, namely; himself, his wife, his two children, his two brothers, his uncle aged seventy-five years who has always assisted in the work, an invalid sister, and eight servants, 600 livres per head	9600
For his own needs and those of his wife and children, incidental expenses in the house such as linen, laundry, furniture etc.	4000
For the rent of a house large enough for his family, his servants, his horses, carriages, and the utensils necessary to his position, the said house being situated so that he is able to carry out orders promptly	4800
Poll tax, formerly 231, now	2048
	———
	27798

Incidental Expenses

Colleagues; when it is a question of summoning them at my own expense, which happens only too often owing to the bad conduct of the servants whom one is forced to employ and who levy toll when they know they are necessary to one.

Perpetual *pourboires* [gratuities], with which one must keep a hold on those whom one requires.

The replacing of horses when they die, and the expense of their illness.

The illness of servants, of whom one must take care, or else one would find no others.

The enormous New Year gifts which one must not fail to give, or there would be no servants the next day.

The expenses on the days when there are executions.

The utensils to be used at executions, which have to be constantly renewed. There are a thousand other incidental expenses which it is impossible to mention in detail because they arise at the moment. All these expenses may be reckoned as a further sum of 5000 livres.

Observations

If the executioner were expected to put the torture, or act as carpenter [i.e. manufacture and maintenance of scaffold etc.], the following expenses would result from the work;
For putting the torture, one extra assistant;
For the carpenter's work three carriages, three horses, their harness, the farrier, the two carters, two assistant carpenters, and a place in which to store the planks and put them together, and to shelter men, horses, carriages and tools;
Timber necessary for repairs;
The upkeep of everything;
Incidental expenses in the country;
The death of horses and expense of replacing them;
All this cannot be estimated at less than 18,000 livres.

I entreat you, Gentlemen, carefully to consider the position of the executioner, in which he is placed by the prejudice that still exists with regard to his calling; and kindly bear in mind that, even when there is no justice to be done, the executioner still has the same expenses, and the same number of people to support and pay; and to satisfy yourselves of the truth of the statement contained in the Memorandum. The facts are authentic.

signed, SANSON
Executioner of Criminal Judgements in Paris

But the Assembly was in no hurry to come to a decision over the executioner's 'pay claim', and while waiting for a favourable response Sanson continued with the duties of his office.

One of those tasks was the execution of the Marquis de Favras, who had been charged with attempting to introduce armed soldiers into Paris with the intention of overthrowing the authorities, stealing the seals of State, and taking away the King and the royal family to sanctuary in Péronne.

Favras, born in 1745, joined the musketeers in 1760 and became lieutenant of the Swiss Guards protecting the King's brother. Marrying in 1774, he resigned his commission and went first to Vienna, then to Holland, where he commanded a legion in the civil insurrections that were taking place in that country.

Unable to quench his thirst for adventure he returned to France and hatched a plan to rescue the King by secretly recruiting an army of 30,000 royalists and then marching on Paris. The details of a scheme on such a grand scale could not possibly have been restricted to just a few conspirators, and the inevitable happened when three of his recruits, Turcati, Marquies and Morel denounced de Favras to the authorities. On Christmas Day 1789 the marquis was arrested by order of the National Assembly.

He was arraigned and brought to trial in the Chatelet prison on 18 February 1790, and from the attitude of the magistrates and the hostile attitude of the public, he realized all hope was lost. On 29 February the verdict was delivered; he was to perform *amende honorable* before the portico of Notre-Dame, and then be hanged.

This method of execution for a marquis was unusual, aristocrats usually having the privilege of dying by the sword. But at that time the legal code was in a state of flux, for the National Assembly was in the process of drawing up a new constitution; moreover a deputy, Dr Guillotin, had put forward proposals to revise extensively all methods of execution (as described in the next chapter).

Even while sentence was being read out in court, Charles-Henri had received orders to erect the scaffold, and so de Favras was led straight out of the prison and on to the tumbril, surrounded by mobs of revolutionists calling for his death. So hectic was the scene that Sanson completely forgot the first part of the sentence; on being reminded, he quickly untied his prisoner's wrists and ordered him to undress. Then, wearing only a shirt and with bare feet – for such minimal apparel was *de rigueur* for the *amende honorable* – de Favras took hold of the taper given to him. Responding to the cries of 'A rope around his neck!', the executioner complied, dropping the hempen noose round the marquis's shoulders.

The procession moved with the greatest difficulty through the multitude until it reached the façade of Notre-Dame. There the marquis took the paper from the clerk and read out the statement of contrition, adding, 'Ready to appear before God, I forgive those who have accused me. I die innocent. Since a victim is needed, it is better that I should die, instead of some innocent man whose courage might fail him in the face of undeserving death. I am about to suffer for crimes which I have not committed.'

When he returned to the cart, Charles-Henri saw that his face was slightly pale but he was clearly retaining his fortitude to the last. The time had now come for the performance of the last act of the tragedy. By now it was dark, and the square was imperfectly lighted, so lanterns had been suspended around the scaffold, transforming the scene into one of shadowy horror. De Favras dismounted from the tumbril and advanced with a firm step. The extraordinary courage he displayed touched some among the howling mob, but his enemies were in overwhelming numbers, and the abuse rose to a deafening crescendo.

On the scaffold Charles-Henri led him to the ladder and steadied it as his victim mounted the rungs, the rope trailing behind him. When he was high enough to be heard by the crowd, he raised his voice and shouted, 'Citizens, I die innocent. Pray for me!' He repeated these words at every step, and when he had climbed nearly to the top of the ladder, he looked up to where the executioner's assistant straddled the arm of the gallows. And as the man bent down to take hold of the rope and attach it to the beam he added, 'And you – do your duty!'

These were his last words. They had hardly passed his lips when, at Sanson's signal, his assistant reached down and turned the ladder, throwing the Marquis de Favras off and leaving his body to twist and swing in the air.

Meanwhile Charles-Henri's financial troubles were increasing; counting on a settlement of his claims, and even perhaps on a return of the old regime, he unavoidably continued to incur debts. But neither event took place and finally, being at the end of his resources, he despatched yet another letter to the procureur-syndic of the department, a note of barely restrained indignation apparent in every line. Only too familiar is his reference to the possibility of pay strikes by his staff, and the difficulty of retaining his best men in the face of competition from the opportunities currently offered by the entrepreneurs flourishing under the new regime.

Letter from executioner Sanson to M. Roederer, attorney-general of the department.

Paris, 6 August 1791

Monsieur,

It is with the greatest respect that I have the honour of explaining my present position to you. It is such that I entreat you, Monsieur, to have the kindness to give me your attention for a moment.

The method of execution that is practised today [i.e., still by the sword and the rope] is expensive, over and above the increase in cost of all the necessities of life. The service of the numerous criminal tribunals forces me to employ a number of persons capable of fulfilling the orders I receive. Since I cannot personally be everywhere at once, I must have people that I can depend on, for the public still demands decency. It is I who pay for that.

To secure the kind of people that are needed for this work, I have to give them double the wages that they asked for in past years. Even then, they came to warn me last Saturday that unless I increased their wages by at least a quarter, they could no longer do the work. The circumstances of the moment forced me to give them a promise.

The removal of the old prejudices (against executioners and their staff, because of the Revolution) seemed at first to have lessened some of the difficulties in the matter of finding assistants; but on the contrary I have found that its only effect was the disappearance of all the men of the class from which I could take them, on account of the facilities they now have for serving private employers, or choosing some other profession, or finding a situation. To secure them therefore I must lure them with the hope of gain.

I have fourteen persons to feed every day, eight of whom receive wages: three horses, three carters, and accessories.

An enormous rent, by reason of my calling; from the earliest times the executioner was always provided with a lodging by the King.

Incidental expenses of executions, now very frequent every day; and other family expenses, such as relatives and old, infirm servants who have sacrificed their lives to this work, and have a right to be treated with humanity.

My present position is this, Monsieur; it is now eight months since I presented the Bureau of Judicial Expenditure an account of my outlay and expenses, which have always been paid to me at the rate of account I furnished; but I cannot succeed in obtaining any of the money; I was very careful, however, to keep within my accustomed charges; I even made reductions myself on several of the entries.

I had the honour, Monsieur, of presenting a request to you on this subject on 11th of last June, without receiving any answer. My financial embarrassment, indeed I may say my considerable debts, make it impossible for me to continue making such important payments, since I no longer know where to look for money. And I cannot apply any more to the persons to whom I owe money, and to whom I cannot return it, if I am not paid myself.

I can only have recourse to yourself, Monsieur, to give orders that I may be paid the money due to me, otherwise it seems that the sacrifices I have made up to the present time, in order that the duties of my office might be correctly performed, will result in the total wreck of my life in this place, and my inevitable ruin by forcing me to abandon my post and my family after twenty-four years of such employment.

As my affairs are urgent I entreat you, Monsieur, kindly to make inquiries of some trustworthy person with regard to the truth that I have the honour of putting before you.

I have that of being, with the most profound respect, Monsieur, Your very humble and obedient servant,

SANSON
Executioner of Criminal Judgements in Paris

But more urgent decisions had to be made by the Assembly, one of them not entirely unrelated to that of Sanson's problems. It concerned the Declaration of the Rights of Man, and specifically the clause which proclaimed that all citizens were equal in life. But what of their rights in death? Were all condemned criminals, whether high-born or peasant, to be executed in the same manner? And if so, by what means? When, later, the question became a burning issue of principle, the problem could well have proved insoluble – until the advent of Dr Guillotin upon the scene.

5 Dr Guillotin and His Device

On 27 May 1738 one of the residents living in the rue Saint Pierre in Saintes, a small town situated in the province of Charente Maritime, left her house for her morning walk. Slowly, for she was eight months pregnant, she crossed the market square, on which had been erected the scaffold. Public executions were commonplace in those days, and she was, no doubt, accustomed to such occurrences. On that particular morning however, the screams of agony uttered by the felon who was being brutally broken on the wheel proved too much for her, and she immediately went into labour. And on the next day Mme Agathe Guillotin gave birth to a son, a boy subsequently christened Ignace Joseph. And such was the manner of his birth that his father, a lawyer, jokingly exclaimed that the executioner had acted as Agathe's midwife!

Joseph, the family's ninth child – they were to have a further three – grew up to be an obedient and God-fearing youth, and when old enough he studied at the local Jesuit college with a view to taking holy orders. He did in fact enter a monastery in Bordeaux, but by the age of twenty-three had decided that the monastic life was not his forte and so he studied for, and obtained, a Master of Arts degree. Thus qualified, he moved to Paris, and enrolled at the School of Medicine, where his diligence and determination earned him the praise of his tutors. On 27 August 1770 he graduated as a doctor of medicine.

Such were his skills that within a matter of months he had attracted a large clientele to his consulting rooms, and become one of the most sought-after and expensive doctors in Paris. Accepted into Paris society, he moved in fashionable circles and played a major part in the establishment of freemasonry in France, holding masonic levees and banquets in the fine town house he had bought and staffed with a large retinue of servants. In appearance Joseph Guillotin was a short, agile man of slight build. Beneath the fashionable wig, *de rigueur* among the Paris gentry, his eyes were dark and deep-set, his nose sharp, his lips full; a man intelligent and ambitious. He dressed

Dr Ignace Joseph Guillotin

elegantly, in a braided three-cornered hat, a black silk coat and lace jabot.

In those early years he seemed to have had little time for women, even apparently going out of his way to shun them. But all this altered when, in 1787, he fell in love. As a collector of fine editions, he was a frequent visitor to the antiquarian bookshop owned by a fellow freemason, Claude-Marie Saugrain, and so became acquainted with the attractive daughter of the family, Marie-Louise.

A tall and nubile woman in her early thirties, she had a devastating effect on Joseph's emotions. The 50-year-old doctor immediately recalled his vanished youth, and blossomed forth in a new outfit. Gone was his usual sombre garb, replaced by a wide-brimmed hat, a long narrow overcoat and a billowing cravat. During the literary discussion groups held by her father, he became more and more encouraged by the lady's long, lingering glances and other signs that she too was attracted to him and, wasting little time, he asked Claude-Marie for her hand in marriage. Consent was gladly given, and so, on 14 July 1787, the happy couple were married in the church of St Victor. Marie-Louise settled down in her new home, her contentment marred only by the fact that she was unable to have children. As the months went by Joseph gave up his career as a doctor, and accepted a new challenge by going into politics.

In the country at large, civil unrest was rife. The Bastille had fallen, the Rights of Man proclaimed. On 5 October 1789 a mob from the city marched on Versailles and brought the royal family back to Paris, where they were virtually imprisoned in the Tuileries Palace. And, active at last in politics, Joseph Guillotin seized the opportunity to express his abhorrence at the inhuman methods of capital punishment still on the statute books, for although the King had abolished torture and the fearsome *questionaire* some years earlier, the gibbet and the gallows, the stake and the hideous penalty of being drawn and quartered, still remained.

Accordingly he presented his proposals in the form of six articles to the other members of the Assembly. Article one stipulated that crimes of the same nature should be punished by the same type of punishment whatever the rank or status of the culprit. Equality for all, even criminals.

The other articles were, briefly, that a criminal's shame should not reflect on his family; his goods and chattels should not be confiscated; his body should be returned to his family or given an ordinary burial; penalties would be exacted against anyone reproaching any of the criminal's family.

The last, and most important article, stipulated that where the death sentence had been pronounced 'the criminal will be decapitated; this will be effected by a simple device'. And in his speech he described how, by means of such a device, 'the mechanism falls like thunder, the head flies, the blood spurts ... the man is no more'. True or false, he is also supposed to have said, 'The penalty I have invented is so gentle that unless a man were expecting to die, he would think that he had felt a slight breeze on the neck....' This is hardly likely to be authentic, for the good doctor never claimed to have invented the device which ultimately bore his name.

At that time the Assembly was engaged in formulating a new constitution, and so only the first of Dr Guillotin's articles was scrutinized, a commission being set up to examine the feasibility of standardization of execution methods. Expert opinion was essential, and who better to consult than the executioner himself? And in view of the fact that the least painful and quickest method of execution to date was that granted as a privilege to members of the upper classes, the question put to Charles-Henri was, 'Couldn't you execute ALL the condemned by the sword, whether they were nobles or commoners?' So clear was the executioner's description of the irrefutable difficulties involved, that his reply is worth quoting in full.

> In order to accomplish the execution in accordance with the intention of the law, it is necessary, even without any opposition on the part of the prisoner, that the executioner should be very competent and the condemned man very steady, otherwise it would be impossible to accomplish an execution with the sword. After each execution the sword is no longer in a condition to perform another, being likely to

break in two; it is absolutely necessary that it should be ground and sharpened afresh if there be several prisoners to execute at the same time. It would be needful therefore to have a sufficient number of swords all ready. This involves very great, almost insurmountable difficulties.

It must further be pointed out that swords have very often broken in the performance of such executions, and the Paris executioner possesses only two, at a cost of 600 livres each.

It must also be taken into account that, when there are several condemned persons to be executed at the same time, the terror produced by this method of execution, owing to the immense amount of blood that is shed and flows everywhere, creates fear and weakness in the hearts of those who are waiting to die, however intrepid they may be. An attack of faintness forms an invincible obstacle to an execution. If prisoners cannot hold themselves up, and yet the executioner proceeds with the matter, the execution becomes a struggle and a massacre.

Even in the case of other executions very far from requiring the accuracy demanded by the sword, one has seen signs of weakness and fear; all this is an argument against execution by the sword.

In other methods of execution it was very easy to hide these signs of weakness from the public because it was not necessary for their accomplishment that a prisoner should be firm and fearless [e.g. when tied to the wheel or at the stake], but with the sword method, if the prisoner moved, the execution failed. How can one control a man who either will not or cannot hold himself still?

By the spring of 1792 no progress had been made to implement Dr Guillotin's proposals. The Assembly, having suspended capital punishment, was getting impatient for a solution to the problem, emphasizing that 'whereas the death penalty be as gentle as possible in its execution, it is decreed that this is a matter of urgency'.

It was then that a medical colleague and friend came to his assistance, a notable surgeon called Antoine Louis, permanent secretary to the Academy of Surgeons. Applying his surgical knowledge to the problem, and carrying out research, he recommended that:

some mechanical means be adopted as in England whereby the body of the criminal is laid between two posts, joined by a cross-beam at the top, whence a convex hatchet is made to fall on the neck by means of a trigger. The beam of the instrument should be heavy and strong enough to act efficaciously, like the ram used for sinking piles in the ground; we know that its force increases in proportion to the height from which it falls.

It is easy to construct such a machine, the effect of which would be infallible. The decapitation would occur instantly, in accordance with the spirit and wishes of the new law. It would be easy to carry out experiments on corpses or even live sheep. It would be seen whether or not it would be necessary to fix the victim's head in a crescent which would embrace the nape of the neck at the base of the skull. The horns, or prolongations of this crescent could be held beneath the scaffold by pins. This apparatus, if it is deemed necessary, would cause no sensation and would hardly be noticed.

In earlier centuries there had indeed been a number of machines similar to that which Louis had in mind. His mention of England referred to the Halifax Gibbet, in use up to 1650, consisting of a blade poised between two uprights, the felon kneeling beneath it. On seeing this machine the Regent of Scotland adopted the idea and had one built in Edinburgh, it being christened the 'Scottish Maiden'.

A much more primitive method was used in ancient China, consisting of a heavy tree trunk about twelve feet in length, hinged at one end to a horizontal beam by means of a large bronze pin, and having a blade protruding from its other extremity. The tree trunk was held vertically by a support which, once the criminal had been secured in position, was knocked away, allowing the trunk to fall with devastating force, the blade severing the felon's head.

Other machines operating in the same general way were thought to have been employed in Ireland in the fourteenth century, in Germany (the 'Diele'), and in Italy ('Mannaia'); even in France itself, the account of the execution of the Maréchal de Montmorency at Toulouse in 1632 described how 'A rope was thrown over his arm and he went to the scaffold, which he reached via a window, for in that country they use an axe which is between two pieces of wood, and when the head is placed on the block, the rope is released and the axe falls and separates the head from the body.'

At length the surgeon's general specifications were passed to M. Guedon, the carpenter whose job it was to manufacture gallows for the government. His description is interesting, albeit somewhat technical.

Estimate for a machine decreed by the National Assembly to serve for cutting the heads of criminals condemned to death, to wit:

The said machine shall consist of two upright posts of new wood of the best quality. They will be eighteen feet in height and equipped with beams hafted with tenons and mortices; for assembly pins will be substituted, pins with a head at one end and screws at the other, with their washers [i.e. bolts].

Ditto. Angle braces hafted with tenons and mortices with grooves above and below, iron pins [i.e. assembly pins].

The said upright posts made to receive the grooves, which will be copper-plated to prevent the wood from swelling and to give speed to the hammer which will pass through them, these also to be of the best quality.

Further, for the scaffold, eight posts of eight feet in length of the best quality young oak, provided with the necessary beams for the framework, above and below and if necessary in the centre, the whole carried out with tenons and mortices, and the pins with heads and screws.

Plus the flooring of the aforesaid scaffold in new oak three inches thick.

Plus the lock of the framework of the aforesaid scaffold to prevent the crowd from standing on it.

For this scaffold, will build a stairway, made up of two oak stringers ten feet long, with twelve steps also in first quality oak, of two inches thick. The whole assembled.

The said stairway three feet wide held at the two ends and in the middle with screws and bolts.

Plus two iron hooks on the upperworks held by two solid screw clamps.

The said stairway provided on each side with a rail, secured with screwed iron flanges.

The total cost quoted was 5,600 livres, but this was rejected by the authorities as exorbitant, despite the contractor's plea that subsequent models would be cheaper. Nor was that the only impediment, for on studying the proposed method, Sanson emphatically stressed that the attitude of the culprit was of great importance and could not be overlooked. It was almost as difficult, he said, for a fainting man to remain on his knees as to stand on his feet. Hanging him, or tying him on the wheel, was possible; but it was hopeless to expect that he would, except in rare cases, remain motionless while the axe descended, even though he was held by the neck. It was then a case of 'back to the drawing board'!

All was not lost however, for by a fortunate chance Sanson had become acquainted with a German engineer called Tobias Schmidt, a manufacturer of mechanical pianofortes and musical instruments. Charles-Henri had purchased some of his instruments and the two men often played duets together, the executioner on the violin, Schmidt on the clavecin, an early type of piano.

On having the principles explained to him, Schmidt immediately roughed out an acceptable design – and the guillotine was born! When constructed it was basically similar to the Halifax Gibbet, for it consisted of two six-inch-thick oak uprights, ten feet high, secured twelve inches apart by a top cross-piece, and mounted on a high base. An inch-deep groove, cut vertically down the inner of each upright, provided channels in which ran the blade. This was six inches in depth and weighed fifteen pounds, with an iron block of up to sixty-five pounds mounted on top to increase the speed of descent.

The blade was originally crescent-shaped but the King, Louis XVI, one of whose hobbies was the study of lock mechanisms, reportedly suggested that it should be of a triangular configuration. The accuracy of his advice was confirmed when, nine months later, it severed his own head.

The blade, or *tranchoir*, was held in the raised position by a rope which passed through a ring at the top of the weighted

JIL

block, both ends passing through brass pulleys mounted high on each upright. The two lengths of rope then hung down the sides of the uprights and were secured there.

A four-inch high block of wood, scooped out to take the victim's neck, was bolted between the base of the uprights. This block, eight inches in width, had a transverse slit across its top to permit the blade to penetrate its depth, ensuring complete separation of head from body. Attached to the block was an iron crescent, the 'lunette', which pressed the victim's neck down on the block and so held the head immovable. One apt phrase at the time was 'to look through the little window', another, as the head fell, being, 'to sneeze into the sack'!

Sanson's concern over the ability of the victim to squirm about while in position was solved very neatly, for the device incorporated a narrow bench extending from the neck block at right angles to the uprights, at the free end of which was hinged a plank, the 'bascule'. On arrival on the scaffold, the victim would be hustled to the bascule, it being in a vertical position, there to be strapped to it, the chief executioner securing his left arm, one assistant his right arm and the other assistant his legs. Instantly the bascule would be pivoted into a horizontal position, slid forward to bring the victim's neck between the two uprights, and the iron lunette dropped into place. If necessary one assistant would stand at the front and pull the victim's hair to stop him attempting to retract his head.

Upon the release of the two ropes, the blade would fall, the severed head then dropping either into a leather bag or a basket lined with oilcloth, the latter being ghoulishly named the 'family picnic basket', and the body would be rolled sideways into a long wicker basket for later conveyance to the cemetery.

The actual operation took far longer to describe than to enact, for Charles-Henri, had he but known it, was to acquire so much expertise in the operation during the coming Revolution, that he was able to despatch no fewer than twelve victims in thirteen minutes, a mercifully quick end for those doomed to die.

But we digress. The device was originally called the

'Louison' or 'Louisette' after Antoine Louis, the surgeon who initially developed Joseph's idea of a 'simple device' into what became an actual machine. It might be said that the credit should have gone instead to the man who, when told what was required, sat down and sketched out the equivalent of a blueprint, and that the machine should therefore have been called the 'Schmidt'; however, Tobias did not lose out, for since his estimate for its manufacture was 824 livres (compared to the 5,600 livres quoted by the government's own carpenter), he received a contract to construct thirty-four of the devices for the provinces, and later went into full-scale production.

Inevitably however, the machine became known as the Guillotine, much to the good doctor's annoyance, especially when, on recognizing him in the streets, citizens would wink at each other and tap the back of their necks! The name had the feminine suffix 'e' added to it, being also known as the 'Widow', because it made so many.

Having finalized the design and completed the construction, the prototype was ready to go into operation. The first tests were carried out on 15 April 1792 by Charles-Henri, using live sheep as specimens. Two days later, assisted by his son Henri, his two brothers Louis Cyr Charlemagne and Louis Charles Martin, and watched by Dr Guillotin, Antoine Louis, other surgeons, and members of the Assembly, further tests were carried out in a small secluded courtyard of the Bicetre hospital, using three cadavers from the morgue, two men and one woman. All lifeless heads were satisfactorily severed; the efficiency of the device had been proved beyond reasonable doubt.

With hindsight it is tempting to conjecture whether the appalling slaughter of so many thousands of the 'enemies of the People', which started only months later, would have taken place, had such a mechanical decapitating machine not been available; could Dr Guillotin's humane principles merely have resulted in even greater bloodshed than had it never been thought of? For such large numbers of decapitations could not possibly have been achieved by Sanson's sword; or would the leaders of the Revolution have employed scores of amateur and totally unskilled sword-wielders from the Paris mob to perform the task, thereby resulting in an even bloodier massacre?

After the successful trials of 'his' machine, Dr Guillotin faded from the judicial scene. Far from being proud of the merciful aspect he had introduced into the elimination of unwanted members of society, he shunned the praise that by rights was due to him, and was never present at an execution.

6   Charles-Henri: The Decapitator

Ten days after the successful tests on the human corpses in the hospital courtyard, the first execution by the guillotine of a living being took place. It was that of a criminal named Nicolas-Jacques Pelletier who, having been found guilty of attacking a traveller with a dagger and robbing him, had had to wait more or less patiently for his judicial demise since December. He might even have been grateful for the delay, knowing that otherwise he was likely to die slowly of strangulation on the rope.

Now, on the afternoon of 25 April 1792, at last all was ready. The scaffold had been reinforced by the carpenter Guedon to take the added weight of the machine and, with the memories of the crowd's reactions when Louschart was to be broken on the wheel still fresh in the minds of the authorities, the commander of the police was ordered by M. Roederer, Procureur-Syndic, to take all necessary precautions;

> The new method of execution, for cutting off the head, will certainly attract a considerable crowd to the Place de Grève and it is advisable to take measures so that no harm comes to the machine. I therefore think it necessary that you order the police present at the execution to remain in sufficient numbers in the square and the approaches after it has taken place, to facilitate the removal of the machine and the scaffold.

Charles-Henri, making his début with his new device, concealed whatever nervousness he may have felt while being under the concentrated gaze of the vast crowd of spectators which had gathered to inspect this revolutionary

Charles-Henri Sanson (artist's impression)

device (just how revolutionary it was would be only too apparent in the months to come). Always the professional, he led Pelletier, who wore a red shirt as required by law, up on to the platform, the felon then being bound to the bascule and pivoted so that his head lay in the required position. The lunette fell, gripping Pelletier's neck; Sanson reached out and released the pendant blade; and the scaffold juddered as, with a crash that reverberated around the square, the weighted knife hurtled down its grooves and came to rest in the block – having severed the head instantly.

A great success, but one which was not altogether applauded by the crowd. Compared with the usual dramatic spectacle of the noose being placed around a felon's throat, the turning of the ladder which he had climbed, followed by the prolonged spectacle of the victim gyrating on the rope as he slowly suffocated to death, this new method was over and done with in seconds, and so lacked considerable entertainment value; 'Give us back our gallows,' they sang in protest, but took no other violent action.

Paris society in general, however, loved the new machine, and in the months that followed, a guillotine craze swept the country. It was nicknamed the 'People's Avenger', the 'Patriotic Shortener' and the 'National Razor', its popularity not being overlooked by manufacturers, who promptly brought out miniature versions as toys for children (resulting no doubt in the gory loss of many a family pet!). Larger versions for adults included dolls resembling unpopular politicians which could be decapitated at the dinner-party table to exude 'blood', this being a liqueur or perfume.

Fashionable women wore gold or silver earrings in the shape of the guillotine, and brooches too bore its image. Bawdy songs were composed, describing in detail the lopping of the heads, the gushing of the blood. Men had wax tablets made, incorporating its impression, with which to seal their letters; school teachers used models of the guillotine to illustrate their lessons on justice and the law, while theatre impresarios wasted no time in staging plays which included at least one, and often several villains apparently meeting their end on full-size guillotines, much to the delight of the audiences.

Someone even conceived the pleasing idea of beheading

all the stone saints that adorned the church façades. The statues in the niches of the old basilica of Notre-Dame all lost their heads. The whiteness of the broken stone contrasted strikingly with the weather-blackened bodies of the statues, and gave an impression of freshly cut flesh, which was regarded by passers-by as delightfully amusing.

Within days of the execution of Pelletier Sanson was busy again, beheading three soldiers, Devitre, Desbrosses and Cachard, who had murdered a tradesman. He was to suffer a more personal tragedy just a few months later when, on 27 August of that year, assisted by his youngest son Gabriel, he was guillotining three assignat forgers, Vimal, Guillot and Sauvade. All went well until the moment when, in accordance with custom, the heads of those executed had to be displayed to the crowd, both as a deterrent and also as proof that those sentenced to death had indeed been executed.

Accordingly Gabriel picked up one head and advanced to the edge of the scaffold. On brandishing the macabre exhibit for all to see, he suddenly lost his footing on the blood-slippery boards and fell over the edge, being killed as his head struck the ground.

The news of this appalling accident was reported in the *Chronique de Paris* of 29 August 1792;

> The execution of three forgers of assignats was accompanied by certain remarkable circumstances; at the same time eleven men and a woman were exposed in the pillory for other crimes, and witnessed this execution. One condemned man, Guillot, fainted, and the Abbé Sauvade had been into town, where he dictated his will quite calmly, but when he saw what had happened on the scaffold his strength deserted him. It seems that one of the sons of the executioner, who was showing one of the heads to the people without paying attention to his feet, fell off the scaffold and fractured his skull on the ground. He is said to be dead. His father showed the most acute grief.

The executioner, in a state of shock, carried the body home, assisted by his other son Henri, the funeral later taking place in the church at St Laurent. As can be imagined, this tragic accident had an impact on Charles-Henri and Marie-Anne from which neither of them ever really recovered, and the executioner's dedication to his calling faltered from that moment. Following that sad occurrence, all scaffolds were henceforth railed in around their sides, as a safeguard.

Meanwhile the affairs of State were worsening by the day. In April 1792 France had declared war on Austria, and in the following month Prussia allied itself with the enemy. The wartime conditions and the ever-present threat of invasion created widespread unrest and revolt among the populace, feelings exacerbated when the Duke of Brunswick, the Prussian commander, threatened dire consequences should any harm befall King Louis XVI and his family. This strengthened the belief among some anarchic factions that Louis had been conspiring against his own country, and so for safety's sake the Assembly moved the royals from the Tuileries Palace into their own building on 10 August 1792, where they were made to listen to a debate in which the King was relieved of all his authority and functions.

No sooner had the move been effected than the mob attacked the guards defending the Tuileries. It was the practice in those days for the monarchs of many countries to recruit foreign troops as bodyguards in order to reduce the risk of assassination or overthrow by disaffected national guards, and France was no exception.

Louis's personal bodyguard was composed of a thousand Swiss Guard, soldiers not to be denigrated by classing them as mercenaries, for they were loyal and devoted to the monarch. Room by room, balcony by balcony, they fought every inch of the way against the thousands of raging fanatics until, completely overwhelmed, they were brutally massacred by the mob. An Englishman, John Moore, who was in Paris at the time, described how

the naked bodies of the Swiss – for they were already stripped – lay exposed on the ground. I saw a great number on the terrace immediately before the palace; some lying single in different parts of the gardens, and some in heaps, one above another. The gardens and adjacent courts were crowded with spectators, among whom there was a

considerable proportion of women, whose curiosity it was
evident was at least equal to their modesty. The bodies of the
National Guard and of the attacking citizens had already
been removed by their friends; only those of the Swiss lay
exposed in that shocking manner. Of about 800 or 1000 of
these, who were yesterday murdered in the Tuileries, I am
told there are not 200 left alive.

When some sanity returned, the bodies of these dedicated
men were given a Christian burial in the Madeleine
cemetery and commemorative arches were erected over
their graves. A memorial, the Lion of Lucerne, was built in
the Swiss city of that name, as a lasting tribute to their
sacrifice.

For greater protection the royal family was moved into the
Temple, a group of ancient buildings comprising a fortress, a
prison and other administration buildings. They were
housed under primitive conditions, their guards going out of
their way to abuse and sneer at 'M. Capet' as His Majesty
was now called, and the owners of adjoining properties hired
out rooms at extortionate rates to sightseers wishing to
watch and gloat over the royal prisoners as they walked in
the Temple gardens.

Now having the whip-hand, the revolutionary leaders,
supported by the vengeful mobs, also ordered the arrest and
imprisonment of the hundreds of aristocratic families and
others denounced by old enemies or spiteful neighbours as
politically suspect or having royalist sympathies, regardless
of age, class or profession. They were incarcerated in the
Conciergerie and other gaols, this being but a temporary
respite before the mass slaughter which was to follow.

Charles-Henri's position at this stage was decidedly
tenuous. As the executioner of the law, the King's law, he
ran the fearsome risk of being regarded as a royalist, and so
being put to death. On the other hand, as a trained and
professional despatcher of criminals, he was, if only for the
time being, indispensable to the new rulers in their avowed
aim of cleansing the nation of the erstwhile ruling classes;
but he would have to tread warily, for even he was not
totally irreplaceable.

And so he made up his mind that he had no alternative but

to continue as Monsieur de Paris, but would also try to alleviate the sufferings of his victims as much as he could. At least, thanks to Dr Guillotin and the others, he now had the very instrument with which to execute his victims as painlessly as possible.

He did not have long to wait before being called on to mount the scaffold again, for the Revolutionary Tribunal sat daily. This judicial body, against whose rulings there was no appeal, was composed of a president and vice president, seventeen judges and five deputy judges, sixty jurymen and a public prosecutor, the infamous Antoine Quentin Fouquier-Tinville.

Dispensing with due legal process, multiple death sentences were passed, the executions of which were to take place the same day. Charles-Henri, dressed in his uniform of a dark-green *redingote* (a long, full-skirted coat) worn with a wide white cravat and striped trousers, a tricorn hat covering his long sandy hair, would go with his assistants to the prison, there to prepare the 'convicts' (as they were then termed) for their rendezvous with the guillotine. Lest hair impede the falling blade, it was cut away, and usually sold to the wigmakers of Paris for profit. A member of the Assembly pointed out sarcastically that;

A new sect has lately been formed in Paris; in their zeal to associate themselves with the revolutionaries by every possible means, they have the same desires, the same sentiments and in these days the same hair; toothless women are eager to buy the locks of any golden haired young spark who has been guillotined, and to wear such tresses on their heads. It is a new branch of commerce, and a perfectly new kind of devotion too. Do not let us interfere with these tender joys; let us respect these blonde wigs; our aristocrats will at least be of some use; their hair will hide the bald heads of a few women....

As well as having their hair cut away, the victims' shirts or blouses were slit down the back and then, with hands tied behind them, their feet bare or wearing slippers, they were loaded into the red-painted tumbrils, seated facing each other and bound to the wooden side-rails of the cart.

To present the spectacle to as many of the inhabitants of Paris as possible, the longest route was usually taken; from the Palais de Justice, across the Pont au Change, via the Quai de la Mégisserie and rue de la Roule, along the rue Saint Honoré, to the Place de la Révolution (today the Place de la Concorde), the journey taking anything from three quarters of an hour to an hour and a half.

As the terrible months passed, the routes were varied as neighbourhoods objected to the convoys of tumbrils, for they completely paralysed trade and caused the shopkeepers to close their shops. First the hawkers would appear, selling the day's fixture list of victims, followed by itinerant traders with baskets of food and refreshments. Spectators would start to assemble, chanting revolutionary slogans and competing for the best vantage points.

At last the tumbrils would appear, escorted by police, the sight of their human cargo evoking jeers and abuse throughout the length of the route.

The square itself heaved with the vast crowds, spectators hanging out of windows and from balconies, soldiers cordoning off the scaffold itself, whilst near the platform stood officers of the Tribunal, clad in black robes over which hung their silver chains of office. And nearby waited the red carts which would be the means of transporting the decapitated bodies to the cemeteries.

On arrival the convicts were lined up at the foot of the steps, where they waited until their names were called out by Charles-Henri, whose uniform was now protected by a bloodstained overall. Most of the doomed victims conducted themselves in a dignified manner, not deigning to heed the catcalls and abuse from the crowd. As each one mounted the scaffold in turn, they were secured to the bascule, which was instantly pivoted forward and downwards, the victim's neck being positioned on the lower part of the collar. The top half was slammed down, so pinning the victim immovable; if necessary one of the assistants would grip the victim's hair (or if he were bald, the ears) and pull, in order to stretch the neck.

Under the watchful eye of Charles-Henri, the release rope was then pulled, allowing the heavy blade to hurtle downwards. As the severed head fell into the waiting basket, blood spurted from the gaping neck, spraying the assistant and flooding across the scaffold boards, to drain through the cracks into the sand-filled pit beneath the scaffold and overflow into the gutters. The torso was quickly rolled sideways into a long wicker basket or makeshift coffin – and the next pitiful victim was then led up the steps.

At intervals the corpses were carted away to the cemeteries, where scenes reminiscent of Dante's *Inferno* were constantly re-enacted. At the edge of the gaping trench, perhaps already three quarters full, officials stripped the headless corpses and flung bunches of them, naked, on top of those delivered earlier. During this operation, wood fires were kept burning, and thyme, sage and juniper were thrown on the flames to mask the appalling stench of decomposing flesh that permeated the air.

Worse was reported by the historian Montgaillard, who averred that 'at Meudon there was a Tannery of Human Skins; such of the Guillotined as seemed worth flaying; of which perfectly good wash-leather was made, for breeches and other uses. The skin of the men was superior in toughness and quality to shamoy [chamois]; that of the women was good for almost nothing, being so soft in texture.'

Regulations concerning the disposal of the victims' apparel varied. At one time the Paris executioner and his staff were allowed to claim them, at other times it was forbidden. This latter ruling provoked a letter submitted by the executioner's assistants and addressed to the public prosecutor:

Citizen; since the Revolution the assistants of Sanson, Executioner of Criminal Sentences of your Tribunal, have always taken away the garments of executed persons. These insignificant articles in themselves can only supplement our salaries to an extent that in these days is not excessive, owing to the kind of work we do. Our clothes are ruined in a very short time, in spite of the precautions we take to prevent in some degree, at all events, the terrible effect that executions have on them.

Having a salary of only 1000 livres, which is however increased by half at the expense of our cousin Sanson, whose assistants we are, it is still impossible for us to meet the expenses that we individually incur in the laborious, painful, dirty tasks that we repeat every day. But then, citizen Chaumet, formerly national agent of the Commune, successfully urged the passing of a resolution by which we were deprived of the clothes of executed prisoners. The accessories still remained to us.

We were informed yesterday evening of a new resolution which forbids us for the future to take possession of anything. As this resolution is not yet law but seems to us to be under consideration, we pray you, citizen, of your kindness, to see that the underlinen, handkerchiefs, boots and shoes etc., are restored to us. Our employment demands great expense. This suppression would make it impossible for us to meet them.

[Signed Demorets, senior]

Demorets, junior

François le Gros

Le Vasseur

[who declared he could not sign his name]

However, this appeal failed, the clothes being declared the property of the Republic, and at the cemeteries the garments and footwear of all the victims were sorted into different heaps, a clerk making an inventory of them. All the blood-caked finery was sent to the river to be washed, and then handed over to the Administration des Hôpitaux for distribution to charitable organizations.

On the many days of the week when executions took place, even a blind person would know whereabouts he was in the city, for only near the Place de la Révolution would he hear the three dreaded sounds symbolic of the Terror; the thump as the bascule was swung horizontally; the clang of the top half of the lunette dropping into place; and the crash as the weighted blade fell.

As mentioned earlier the actual procedure took place in far fewer seconds than it takes to recount it. The rate of despatch almost defies belief, for at the height of the bloodbath Charles-Henri and his team were decapitating nearly one a minute, most of this time being taken by having to assist each bound victim up the steps; 300 men and women were slaughtered in three days, 1,300 in six weeks; and between 8 and 27 July 1794 no fewer than 600 were decapitated on the Paris scaffold.

A letter sent by a deputy of the Commune to the Committee of Public Safety showed the pride felt in the capital at Sanson's expertise; revealed too the underlying savagery:

> I shall always point to Paris, for Paris can serve as a universal model. In Paris the art of guillotining has reached the pitch of absolute perfection. Sanson and his pupils guillotine with celerity, so swiftly do they conjure their man out of the way; they once despatched a dozen in thirteen minutes.
>
> Send the chief executioner of Marseilles to Paris, then, to take a course of guillotining from Sanson, or we shall never be finished. You may be sure that we will never leave you in need of prey for the guillotine, and that a great number must be despatched. The promptitude of the guillotine must be supplemented in ways that will stimulate the people's minds when their enemies are taken to the scaffold. It must be made into a sort of spectacle for them. The aristocrats must be shown, by songs and dances, that their death is the people's only happiness. And in addition to this it must be contrived that there shall be a great concourse of people to accompany them to the scaffold.

And celebrations there were. On special occasions the scaffold in the Place de la Révolution was surrounded by as many wooden posts as there were *départements* in the Republic, each being surmounted by a shield on which the name of the *département* was inscribed, and round them the people sang and danced.

Such were the numbers to be executed that the General Council of the Commune gave orders that the guillotine should remain in place overnight 'with the exception of the blade, which the chief executioner shall be empowered to remove every evening'. The instrument would, in any case, require cleaning and sharpening in readiness for the next day's batch of victims.

Sickened by the slaughter, the executioner worked like an

automaton, keeping the production belt of death constantly on the move, knowing full well that should he refuse, he too would pay the price, and others less merciful than him would take over. This possibility was in fact pointed out to him on one occasion by Fouquier-Tinville, the all-powerful prosecutor, who demanded to know why Charles-Henri himself did not pull the rope which caused the death blow to be delivered. The executioner agreed that when the sword was in use, it was customary for the executioner to perform sentences requiring decapitation, but that since a machine had been substituted for human strength and dexterity, the most important duty was the preparation and performance of the execution. The slightest neglect could give rise to frightful accidents, and as he was personally responsible, it was natural that he should concentrate on superintending the execution.

This apparently satisfied Fouquier-Tinville, but he warned Charles-Henri that he would keep an eye on him, adding, with a significant gesture, that if he did not discharge his duties, not only as an experienced executioner, but also as a patriot, he, Sanson, might well change places and be executed himself! Ironically, some months later, the tide of the political parties changed so violently that, as will be related, Fouquier-Tinville himself was condemned to death – and lost his head on Sanson's guillotine!

At heart, Charles-Henri was a royalist, but in the prevailing political climate it would have been suicidal to have shown where his sympathies lay. And so it came as an overwhelming shock when, on 20 January 1793, he was instructed to erect a scaffold for the execution of King Louis XVI on the following day. The order itself gave him little vital information; was he to collect the King and bring him, hands tied behind his back, in the usual tumbril? Were there any special burial arrangements? Seeking urgent clarification he immediately sent a letter back by messenger:

To the Procureur-general
Citizen; I have just received the orders you sent me. I will adopt all measures necessary to prevent any delay in carrying them out. The carpenter has been informed of the position

required for the machine, which will be set up at the spot indicated.

It is absolutely necessary that I should know how Louis will leave the Temple prison. Will he have a carriage or will it be in the vehicle ordinarily used for executions of this kind? After the execution, what will become of the dead man's body?

Is it I or my assistants who must be at the prison at eight o'clock, as is stated on the order? In the case of its not being myself, who must bring him from Temple, what is the place and the exact point at which I am to be?

Since all these things are not mentioned in the order, it would be well if the citizen acting for you would supply me as quickly as possible with this information, while I am engaged in giving all the orders necessary to ensure that everything shall be punctually carried out.

Paris, 20 January 1793, year 2 of the French Republic.
Citizen Sanson,
Executioner of Criminal Sentences

His queries did not include any mention of the need to 'prepare' the King by having his hair cut at the back of the neck; either Charles-Henri had overlooked this in his haste to get everything ready, or had assumed that it would not be necessary, for Louis usually wore his hair tied back with a ribbon, which could be moved forward out of the way once the royal victim had been positioned beneath the knife.

On the same day he also received anonymous letters, some begging him not to despatch the monarch, and one informing him that plans had been made to rescue the King during the journey from the Temple prison to the Place de la Révolution; that he should delay the execution for as long as possible so as to give time for a number of resolute men to break through the cordon of militia and carry off the King. The letter went on to warn him that if he offered any resistance, he would be killed.

An escape bid had actually been made some two years earlier when the royal family had fled in a cumbersome travelling carriage, a newly-built, yellow-painted large 'Berline' driven by the Comte Axel de Fersen, an officer in the Royal Swedish Regiment. Arrangements had been made between the Queen, Marie Antoinette, and her brother Leopold II of Austria, the latter promising that, if the attempt proved successful, money and troops would be forthcoming to march on Paris and restore the sovereignty.

Everything had been planned, troops of Dragoons and Hussars with fresh horses had been stationed at intervals along the route to replace those pulling the heavy Berline, and the members of the royal party had adopted new identities, the children's governess, Mme de Tourzel, pretending to be 'Baronne de Korff', while Marie Antoinette was disguised as the family's governess. The young Dauphin wore little girl's clothes and was addressed as 'Amelie', and Madame Elizabeth became a nursery maid, 'Aglie'. The King himself adopted the unusual disguise of a valet, and the coach was escorted by three Life Guards masquerading as servants, clad in yellow uniforms.

But the schedule soon became disrupted. Capable of travelling at only about three miles an hour via a circuitous route to avoid large towns, delays were caused by the need to effect repairs when a wheel struck a bridge. And the presence of some detachments of troops with fresh supplies had so alarmed local villagers that the militia had been summoned, the troops having to abandon their operation lest the plan be revealed.

Disaster struck when a halt was made to change horses at the post tavern in the small village of Sainte Menehould. The Dauphin was suffering from the heat, and so the carriage windows had been lowered, but the green curtains not drawn together. The innkeeper, an ex-dragoon named Jean-Baptiste Drouet, on seeing the passengers in the white leather interior of the vehicle, thought that the man purporting to be a valet bore an unmistakable resemblance to the King, and confirmed it by glancing at the portrait on the assignat he had just received in payment for the fresh horses he had supplied. As Napoleon was later to say prophetically, 'That glance changed the face of the world.'

Having no local militia to call on in the village, Drouet waited until the coach had departed; then together with a companion, Guillaume, also an ex-dragoon, he rode across country to arouse the villagers along the route, while the Berline headed ponderously towards Varennes, where another relay of troops with fresh horses would be waiting.

There, however, the troops had had to camp a few hundred yards outside the village and, the royal party being six hours late, their officer, Boullie, had gone to bed, the horses were 'at hay', and the escort of Hussars were drinking in the local taverns.

After a fruitless search the Berline started off again, only to find that Drouet's efforts to raise the alarm had been successful; the bridge over the river Aire had been blocked by wagons, barrows, even barrels, and armed militia lined the road – the game was up.

Officials from Paris were sent for, and the royal party was escorted back to the capital by Antoine Pierre Joseph Marie Barnave and Jerome Petion de Villeneuve, they having the audacity to ride in the royal coach. It was even reported that de Villeneuve ate his luncheon therein, drinking wine and throwing his chicken bones out of the window past the royal noses!

As the would-be escapees were escorted back into captivity through the crowded streets, they were greeted, not with triumphant jeers or abuse, but by a sullen silence, as a result of the placards widely displayed which stated, 'Whoever applauds the King shall be flogged; whoever insults him shall be hanged.'

On the day the King was to die, Charles-Henri described the mounting tension he felt over the coming ordeal:

On the morning of the execution I started out at seven o'clock, after embracing my poor wife whom I did not expect to see again. I took a fly [a horse-drawn carriage] with my brothers Charlemagne [then executioner of Provins] and Louis Martin [executioner of Tours]. The crowd was so large in the streets that it was close on nine o'clock before we reached the Place de la Révolution. Gros and Barre, my assistants, had erected the guillotine, and I was so convinced that it would not be used that I hardly looked at it. My brothers were well armed, and so was I; as well as our swords, we had, under our coats, daggers, four pistols and a flask of powder, and our pockets were full of bullets. We felt sure that some attempt would be made to rescue the King, and we intended, if we could, to assist in saving his life.

When we reached the square, I looked about me for my son Henri [then serving with the army] and I discovered him at a short distance away, with his battalion. He nodded and seemed to encourage me. I listened intently for some indication as to what was about to occur. I rejoiced at the thought that the King had perhaps been rescued on the way, and that he was already beyond the reach of danger.

As however my eyes were bent in the direction from which the procession would approach, I suddenly espied a body of cavalry coming at a trot, and immediately after it, a carriage drawn by two horses and surrounded by a double row of horsemen. No doubt could now exist; the victim was at hand. My sight became dim, and I looked at my son; he also was deadly pale.

The carriage stopped at the foot of the scaffold. The King was sitting on the back seat to the right; next to him was his confessor, and on the front seat sat two gendarmes. The latter came down first; then the priest stepped out, and he was directly followed by the King, who appeared even more cool and calm than when I saw him at Versailles and in the Tuileries.

As he approached the steps of the scaffold I cast a last glance around. The people were silent, the drums were sounding, and not the slightest sign of a rescue being at hand was given. Charlemagne was as troubled as I was; as to my brother Martin, he was younger and had more firmness. He advanced respectfully, took off his hat, and told the King that he must take his coat off. 'There is no necessity,' answered he. 'Despatch me as I am now.' My brother insisted, and added that it was indispensably necessary to bind his hands.

This last observation moved him greatly. He reddened and exclaimed, 'What! Would you dare to touch me? Here is my coat, but do not lay a finger on me!' After this he took off his coat. Charlemagne came to his brother's assistance and, scarcely knowing how to address the illustrious victim, he said in a cold tone which hardly concealed his profound emotion, 'It is absolutely necessary; the execution cannot proceed otherwise.'

In my turn I intervened and, bending close to the ear of the priest, I whispered, 'Monsieur l'Abbé, ask the King to submit. While I tie his hands we can gain time, and perhaps some assistance may be forthcoming.'

The abbé looked sadly and hopefully in my face, and then addressed the King. 'Sire,' he said. 'Submit to this last sacrifice, which shall make you look more like our Saviour.' The King held out his hands while his confessor was presenting a crucifix to his lips. Two assistants then tied the hands that had held a sceptre. He then ascended the steps of the scaffold, supported by the worthy priest. 'Are these drums going to sound for ever?' he said to Charlemagne. On reaching the platform he advanced to the side where the crowd was thickest, and made such an imperative gesture that the drummers stopped for a moment.

'Frenchmen!' he exclaimed in a strong voice. 'You see your King ready to die for you! May my blood cement your happiness – I die innocent of what I am charged with!' He was about to continue when Antoine Joseph Santerre, the National Guard commander in charge of the proceedings, ordered the drummers to beat, and nothing more could be heard.

In a moment the King was bound to the bascule, and a few seconds afterwards, while under my touch the knife was sliding down, the victim still could hear the priest pronouncing these words: 'Son of Saint-Louis, ascend to Heaven!'

Thus died the unfortunate prince, who might have been saved by a thousand well-armed men; and really I am at a loss to understand the notice which I had received the day before the execution, that some attempt at rescue would be made. The slightest signal would have been sufficient to cause a diversion, for if, when Gros, my assistant, showed the King's head to the multitude, some cries of triumph were uttered, many of the crowd turned away with profound horror.

Security was certainly massive, the authorities being determined not to take the slightest risk of an escape bid. With rumours circulating that more than 6,000 persons had been hired to attempt to wrest Louis XVI from death, the route planned from the prison to the scaffold site went via wide and open roads and so was easily guarded. The King's

King Louis XVI

carriage was escorted by between 12 and 15,000 well-armed men, and over 100,000 more were ranged in impenetrable rows lining the boulevards. Cannon were stationed at regular intervals, and orders were issued to close all the side-roads at every junction.

Interesting as it is to have the executioner's version of what happened that day, an account from an entirely different and contrasting viewpoint was given by the King's confessor, Abbé Firmont, who said:

I got in the coach and sat down next to His Majesty, facing

the two gendarmes who, it was said, had orders to kill him if they observed the least movement amongst the spectators. I do not know if this was true, but it seems to me that unless they had other arms on them than those which were visible, it would have been extremely difficult to carry out such a design, for they seemed to have only muskets, which it would have been impossible to use. The movement that was feared was not altogether imaginary; a large number of persons devoted to the King had determined to snatch him by force from the hands of the executioners, or at least dare all with that intent. Two of the leaders, young men of a very well known name, had come to warn me of this the day before, and without being entirely convinced, I did not give up all hope until we reached the very foot of the scaffold.

I have since learned that the orders of the Commune for that terrible morning had been so carefully conceived and so rigidly executed, that of the four or five hundred persons who had sworn to attempt a rescue, only twenty-five were able to reach the rendezvous at the Porte St Denis. There, four royalists with raised swords managed to break through the cordon, shouting 'Come on, Frenchmen! Help us save the King!' But no one responded, and the soldiers gave chase. One, de Batz, escaped, but the other three were cut down in the rue de Clery. All the rest of the would-be rescuers, by reason of the measures taken throughout the city, could not even leave their houses.

The King, finding himself shut in a coach where he could neither speak to me nor hear me without witnesses to our conversation, kept silent. I handed him my breviary, the only book I had with me. He gratefully accepted it; he seemed to wish me to point out the psalms which were best suited to the occasion, and recited them alternately with me. The gendarmes, also remaining silent, seemed amazed at the calmness and piety of a monarch whom they had no doubt never seen so close at hand before.

The drive lasted nearly two hours. All the streets were lined with citizens, armed, some with pikes and some with muskets. The coach itself was surrounded by a large body of troops, no doubt drawn from the most corrupt and revolutionary in Paris. As an added precaution a number of drummers marched in front of the horses in order to prevent any shouts being heard that might be raised in the King's favour. But there were no shouts; not a soul was to be seen in the doorways or in the windows; no one was in the streets save those armed citizens who, no doubt through fear and weakness, connived at a crime which perhaps many of them detested in their hearts.

The coach arrived, amid a great silence, and stopped in the middle of a wide empty space which had been left around the scaffold; this space was edged with cannon, and beyond, as far as the eye could see, one saw an armed multitude.

As soon as the King felt the coach coming to a stop, he leaned over to me and said in a whisper, 'We have arrived, if I am not mistaken.' My silence said yes. One of the executioners came forward to open the door of the coach, and as soon as he had got out, three of the executioners surrounded him and tried to remove his outer clothing. He pushed them away with dignity and took off his coat himself.

The executioners, disconcerted for a moment by the King's proud bearing, recovered themselves and surrounded him again in order to bind his hands. 'What are you doing?' said the King, quickly drawing his hands back. 'Binding your hands,' answered one of them. 'Binding me!' said the King in a voice of indignation, 'Never! Do what you have been ordered, but you shall never bind me.' The executioners insisted; they spoke more loudly, and seemed to be about to call for help to force the King to obey.

This was the most agonizing moment of this terrible morning; one minute more, and the best of kings would have received an outrage a thousand times worse than death, by the violence that they were going to use towards him. He seemed to fear this himself and, turning his head, seemed to be asking my advice. At first I remained silent, but when he continued to look at me, I said, with tears in my eyes, 'Sire, in this new outrage I see one last resemblance between Your Majesty and the God who is about to be your reward.'

At these words he raised his eyes to heaven with an expression of unutterable sadness. 'Surely,' he replied, 'it needs nothing less than His example to make me submit to such an insult.' Then turning to the executioners he exclaimed, 'Do what you will; I will drink the cup, even to the very dregs.'

The steps of the scaffold were extremely steep. The King was obliged to lean on my arm, and from the difficulty they caused him, I feared that his courage was beginning to wane; but what was my astonishment when, arrived at the top, he let go of me, crossed the scaffold with a firm step, silenced with a glance the fifteen or twenty drummers who had been placed directly opposite, and in a loud voice pronounced these unforgettable words: 'I die innocent of all the crimes with which I am charged. I forgive those who are guilty of my death, and I pray God that the blood which you are about to shed may never be required of France.' He was continuing, when a man on horseback, in the national uniform, and with a ferocious cry, ordered the drummers to take up the beat again. Many voices were at the same time heard encouraging the executioners. They seemed reanimated themselves, in seizing with violence the most virtuous of kings; they dragged him under the axe of the guillotine, which with one stroke severed his head from his body.

All this passed in a moment. The youngest of the executioners, who seemed about eighteen, immediately seized the head and showed it to the people as he walked round the scaffold; he accompanied this monstrous ceremony with the most atrocious and obscene gestures. At first an awful silence prevailed; at length some cries of '*Vive la République!*' were heard. By degrees the voices multiplied, and in less than ten minutes this cry, a thousand times repeated, became the universal shout of the multitude, and every hat was in the air.

The body was placed in a long wicker basket and taken on the executioner's cart to the Madeleine cemetery, where a trench six feet wide and ten feet deep had already been dug, a cartload of quicklime standing nearby. The body of the King was not taken into the church. After a brief absolution two priests accompanied it, now in a pinewood coffin, to the grave-side, escorted by a crowd of onlookers kept in order by dragoons and gendarmes, while the band played rousing republican tunes.

Abbé Renard recited the prayers for the dead over the body, which was dressed in a waistcoat of white pique, with grey silk breeches and stockings. The hat, a little three-cornered one to which had been fastened a new national cockade, and the shoes, were missing. The head was laid between the legs, the face was not discoloured in any way, and the eyes were wide open. The corpse having been covered with quicklime, the coffin was duly lowered into the trench and the earth filled in.

When the cart returned to the Place de la Révolution, the wicker basket fell to the ground and was immediately surrounded by the gloating mob who soaked handkerchiefs and pieces of cloth in the King's blood, one man even rubbing a pair of dice over the bloodstained wickerwork.

Far from rejoicing, Charles-Henri felt nothing but remorse at having to kill a king (as did Richard Brandon, the executioner of Charles I of England, a century and a half earlier), and, unusually for him, after returning home he left abruptly and did not return until two o'clock in the morning. His wife, concerned by his absence and aware how troubled his conscience was by having to guillotine the King, was relieved when he explained that he had sought out a fugitive priest and, with two nuns who had escaped from a Carmelite convent, had celebrated an expiatory mass for the soul of the dead monarch.

Exactly what had happened was kept a secret until after his death, when Marie-Anne and their son Henri divulged all to the French novelist Honoré de Balzac. The account reveals the mental turmoil suffered by Charles-Henri at that time, remorse that could only be alleviated by some gesture of forgiveness by the Church, something with which he could expunge the overwhelming feelings of guilt that assailed him.

He found his way to the derelict house in which the priest and his companions had taken refuge from the authorities and there, in a room sparsely furnished with straw mats on the floor and containing only a table and a couch, he voiced his request. The events which took place that cold January night are described by Balzac:

> Charles-Henri said, 'Father, I come to beseech you to say a mass for the repose of the soul of a person whose body shall never be buried in hallowed ground.'
> The priest scanned the stranger's features. Evident anxiety

could be seen there, and his looks were anxious and pleading. 'Well,' replied the priest, 'return at midnight; I shall then be ready to celebrate the only funeral service we can offer in expiation of crime.'

Sanson bowed respectfully and, grateful at the reception he had received, left the house. At midnight he returned, to find that the nuns had placed a chest of drawers in the centre of the room, over which was draped an altar-like covering of green moire. A large crucifix of ebony and ivory hung from the wall, and four small thin tapers which the sisters had fixed with yellow wax upon the improvised altar furnished a pale and flickering light. These tapers hardly lighted the other parts of the room, but it made the holy objects discernible and thereby looked like rays from Heaven on this unadorned altar.

The floor was damp. The roof, which steeply descended on both sides as is usual in garrets, was cracked, and an icy wind penetrated through the openings. Nothing could be less pompous and yet, never was anything more impressive than this gloomy ceremony.

The two old nuns were kneeling on either side of the altar, joining in the prayers of the priest who, clad in his pontifical vestments, was holding up a gold pyx studded with precious stones, a sacred vase saved no doubt from the pillage of the Abbey of Chelles. Then, next to this vessel, the wine and the water reserved for the holy sacrifice were contained in two glasses scarcely worthy of the lowest wine shop. As he had no missal, the priest placed his breviary on a corner of the altar. A common plate was provided for the laving of the innocent and bloodless hands.

The stranger piously knelt between the two nuns, and they celebrated an 'Obit', without the body of the defunct, interceding with God for a king of France, and going through a funeral service without his coffin. The whole monarchy was there, in the prayer of a priest and two poor women; and perhaps the Revolution was also represented by Sanson, this man whose face betrayed too much remorse not to make believe that he was actuated by boundless repentance. And when the Pater Noster was said, tears came to the stranger's eyes; to this prayer the priest added, 'And forgive the regicides as Louis XVI himself forgave them.'

After the mass for the dead had been recited, the service was terminated and the two nuns retired. Still unaware of the stranger's identity but assuming him to be one of those timorous members of the Convention who had sacrificed a royal head in order to preserve their own, he said gently, 'My son, if you dipped your hands in the blood of the King, confide in me – there is no fault that cannot be forgiven by a repentance so sincere and touching as yours.'

Charles-Henri paused, then answered, 'Father, none is more innocent of the crime than I am.' He went on, 'I cannot offer an ordinary fee for the funeral service you have just celebrated for the repose of the soul of the King and the quietude of my conscience. An invaluable boon can only be returned by an equally invaluable offering. Deign to take, therefore, this gift of a holy relic. A day shall come when you will understand its value.'

Sanson then gave the priest a small box, and went on to explain that he would do all in his power to protect the fugitives from arrest. Before taking his departure he said quietly, 'A year hence, on 21 January, if you remain here, I shall return and celebrate another expiatory mass.'

When he had gone, the priest placed the box on the table and Mademoiselle de Charost, unable to control her curiosity any longer, opened it. Within was a rather large pocket-handkerchief of very fine cambric. It was soiled by a few drops of perspiration. After looking at it with scrupulous attention, they found a number of small dark spots, as if the cambric had received splashes. 'It is blood!' exclaimed the priest in a deep voice, and reverently placed it on the altar.

During the following weeks and months the nuns found linen and garments secretly delivered to their dwelling, supplied by Sanson's wife Marie-Anne; provisions and wood and, even more essential, *cartes de civisme*, identity cards issued by the authorities as evidence of political integrity, without which one could go nowhere without being challenged, even being necessary in order to buy food.

On 21 January 1794 Sanson returned again, to celebrate the expiatory mass; this practice he continued each anniversary until the Revolution ended and public worship was re-established by the First Consul Napoleon.

The handkerchief given to the priest was of course that of the King, Louis having used it to mop his brow whilst in the carriage. A few drops of blood had splashed on it when his head fell into the basket.

Some of the King's garments were claimed by the executioner's assistants, the puce coat being cut into tiny fragments and, enclosed in rings, sold as souvenirs. The royal shoes, missing at the time of burial, together with a collar buckle, were retained by Charles-Henri, and the family were only induced to part with them under exceptional circumstances.

A few days after the King's death a horseman, followed by a servant, came to the Sanson house. Charles-Henri was out, and so Henri received the visitor. He was a man of elegant appearance, dressed in black, and when asked the purpose of his visit, he replied, 'Sir, I am told that you possess different objects which once belonged to the late King. As I suppose you wish to sell them, I came to make you an offer.'

Henri, indignant at the man's mercenary attitude, exclaimed, 'We have, as you say, kept a few articles belonging to the late King, but we owe no explanations to anyone concerning the use we intend to make of them; and I may as well tell you at once that we do not propose to part with them at any price.'

The visitor looked surprised. 'What! If I offered you a princely ransom for your prize....'

Henri interrupted him. 'We would not accept it,' he rejoined curtly.

While he was speaking, Henri looked closely at the visitor, and was struck by the resemblance the man bore to Louis XVI; the same aquiline nose, high forehead and thick lips, all the typical features of the Bourbons. The visitor glanced round the room and, seeing on the wall a fine engraving of Louis XV, dated 1733, an expression of surprise appeared on his face.

'If you knew,' he said, 'on what grounds I ask for these melancholy souvenirs, perhaps you would not refuse to let me have them. Let me inform you that I belong, by a secret relationship, to the family of the royal victim. I am the son of the King portrayed there, and I am usually styled the Abbé de Bourbon.'

Henri Sanson looked at the portrait; the likeness was obvious. The Abbé de Bourbon was one of the illegitimate sons of that monarch, offspring who were far too numerous to be legally recognized. Secretly protected by Louis XVI, this son had been able to lead a semi-princely life and so felt a deep sense of gratitude towards his benefactor.

Henri, understanding the man's natural desire to possess some remembrance, however small, of his dead relative, could not resist his entreaties. Accordingly he took the shoes and collar buckle from the cupboard in which they were kept, and presented them to the visitor, declining to accept any remuneration other than the abbé's grateful thanks.

Royalty and members of the aristocracy might die, but death also stalked the leaders of the Revolution. On 9 July 1793 a young girl, Marie-Anne Charlotte de Corday d'Aumont, left her home in Caen with the intention of killing Jean-Paul Marat, a revolutionary leader who believed that only the use of force would bring about the necessary changes in the nation's fortunes. Far from being a royalist, she supported the Girondists, a political group dedicated to a more moderate approach to the country's dire problems, and she was filled with a republican fanaticism so intense that she regarded the extermination of Marat as the only solution.

She arrived in Paris on the 11th, and stayed at the Inn de la Providence on the rue des Vieux Augustins. There she wrote a note and despatched it to her quarry, requesting an interview. During the next two days, while waiting for a reply, she visited a cutler's shop on the Palais Royal, where for two francs she purchased a large sheath-knife with an ebony handle. No reply being forthcoming by the 13th, she visited Marat's house and by emphasizing the urgency of her business, was at length admitted to his presence. Marat had been ill for some time. During his earlier revolutionary days he had twice to flee to London, and once had even had to take refuge from the authorities by hiding in the Paris sewers. In those noisome and pestilential tunnels he had contracted a virulent and incurable disease which covered his body in a pruriginous rash so devastating that only almost continual immersion in a sulphur bath brought any relief. Accordingly he spent most of his time in a slipper bath, decency being preserved by a cloth draped over it. With the aid of a board placed athwart the tub, he was able to write his notes and correspondence.

Charlotte Corday approached her prey and, even as he started to query the reason for her visit, she suddenly leant over and plunged the knife into him with all the force she could muster. So violent was the blow that, according to the post-mortem, the blade entered his chest between the first and second ribs, piercing the upper part of the right lung and the aorta, and penetrating the heart, blood gushing copiously into the bath water.

Having achieved her purpose, the young girl made no attempt to escape but stood calmly by the window where, attracted by Marat's dying shriek, she was found by an assistant, Laurent Bas, Marat's mistress Simone Evrard and her sister Catherine.

Faced with the spectacle of his chief semi-submerged in a bath of blood, Bas promptly picked up a chair and knocked Charlotte Corday to the ground; as she attempted to get up, he knocked her down again, detaining her until members of the national guard arrived, accompanied by a surgeon. The body of the murdered man was lifted out and moved on to a bed, and the girl, calm and dignified, her hands tied behind her, was escorted to the Prison de l'Abbaye for interrogation and subsequent trial before the Revolutionary Tribunal. The verdict and sentence were foregone conclusions, the guillotine being the only possible penalty.

In her cell in the Conciergerie a painter, Hauer, who had already started a sketch of her, came and asked whether he might continue with the picture, a request to which she consented. Meanwhile Charles-Henri arrived at the prison to prepare and collect his victim, first speaking to Richard the gaoler and his wife. He commented that she appeared pale and unwell. 'Wait a moment,' the woman replied, 'and perhaps your heart will fail you too.'

Richard then conducted him to the condemned cell. There, guarded by a gendarme, Charlotte awaited him. Cool and entirely composed, she placed a chair in the middle of the floor and, removing her cap, sat down and permitted the executioner to crop her hair. When he had finished she gave a lock or two of it to the artist, and the rest to Richard, requesting him to give it to his wife.

Charles-Henri, marvelling at her serenity, handed her the red shirt which she was to wear, and as he prepared to pinion her hands she asked whether she might keep her gloves on, because her previous captors had bound her wrists so tightly that the cords had chafed her tender flesh. With kind reassurance the executioner told her that she could indeed keep them on, adding that even if she did not, he would make sure that he didn't cause her any discomfort. Charlotte smiled at him. 'To be sure, you ought to know how to do it!' she exclaimed, and held out her bare hands for him to secure her.

The tumbril held two chairs, and when she declined the offer to sit down, Sanson agreed, pointing out that the jolting of the cart over the rough cobbles was less trying while standing, and the procession then set off through the crowds already assembled along the route.

Charles-Henri admitted being unable to take his eyes off his prisoner. He wrote

> The more I saw of her, the more I wished to see. It was not on account of her personal beauty, great as that was; but I thought that it was impossible that she could remain so calm and courageous as I saw her; yet what I hitherto considered as beyond the strength of human nerve actually happened. During the two hours I spent in her company I could detect no sign of anger or indignation on her face. She did not speak; she looked, not at those who insulted her, but at the citizens who were at the windows. The crowd was so dense that our cart advanced very slowly. As I heard her sigh, I said, 'You find the way very long, I fear?' She replied, 'No matter; we are sure to reach the scaffold sooner or later.'

On reaching the Place de la Révolution, the executioner stood in front of her to screen the sight of the guillotine from her gaze, but she insisted on looking, saying, 'I have a right to be curious; this is the first time I see it!'

On dismounting, Sanson noticed that some of the spectators had mingled with his assistants, and as he and the gendarmes were clearing the area, Charlotte briskly ascended the scaffold steps. As she reached the platform

Fermin, one of the executioner's assistants, removed her neckerchief and, without any prompting, she approached the machine and positioned herself on the bascule. Charles-Henri, not wanting to prolong the girl's ordeal longer than absolutely necessary, signalled to Fermin to pull the rope. He did so, and the waiting basket received the head of one of the bravest women Sanson had ever met.

Even as he stood there, a carpenter named François le Gros, picked up the head and showed it to the crowd. Sanson admitted that

> Although I was used to that occurrence, this time I could not help turning my head away. It was then, by the murmurs of the crowd, that I became aware that the rascal had also slapped the cheeks, the face turning red as if insulted. I struck the man, and ordered him off the scaffold, the police taking him away. He was later arrested by the Tribunal and severely punished.
>
> When I went home, the prediction made by Richard's wife came true, for as I was sitting down, Marie-Anne exclaimed, 'What is the matter? Why are you so pale?'

Since 10 August 1792 the royal family had been incarcerated in the Temple prison; the King and his Queen, his sister Mme Elizabeth, and his two children, Mme Royale aged fifteen, and the Dauphin, aged eight. On 21 January 1793 the King had been disposed of; now, in October, it was the turn of the Queen, Marie Antoinette. And whereas the hatred of the Parisians had been directed at the King, rather than the man himself, the Queen was hated as a woman, not only because she was an Austrian, one of the enemy, but because of her independent mind, her extravagant taste, and the lavishness of the royal court she had presided over, the members of which had squandered the nation's finances without thought or consideration. Graft and self-indulgence had been the order of the day; banquets and balls the occupations of the nights. Five hundred flunkeys, servants and menials were employed in the palaces, two thousand horses were housed in the royal stables, hundreds of carriages filled the royal mews, all paid for by the crippling taxes levied mainly on the peasants. Accused of treason,

Queen Marie Antoinette

even of committing incest with her young son; never was a woman more vilified by the people, and few indeed regretted the sentence of death eventually passed upon her by the Revolutionary Tribunal.

Ironically the festivities at her betrothal to the then Dauphin had been accompanied by violence. During the procession, scaffolding had collapsed and 133 people were crushed or trampled to death – and now she too was to end her life violently on a scaffold.

Charles-Henri had been present at the trial and no sooner had the verdict been given than he presented himself before the Public Prosecutor Fouquier-Tinville who wasted no time in asking if preparations for the 'fête' had been completed. As coldly as he dared, Sanson replied that his duty was to await the sentence and not to anticipate it, and was forthwith reprimanded by his superior. Changing the subject, the executioner then asked for the authority to procure a closed carriage, similar to that used by the King on his last journey, in which to convey the Queen to the scaffold. This request infuriated the prosecutor even further; ominously he exclaimed that the executioner himself deserved to perish on the scaffold for daring to make such an insolent suggestion – a common cart was entirely adequate for the Austrian woman.

Having to guillotine the King was traumatic enough; but that he should now have to behead the Queen as well was almost too much for him. Aware of his own outraged emotions, and the tearful reactions of his wife when he told her what he had to do, Charles-Henri realized that he would need some measure of moral support in carrying out the task, and so he enlisted the help of his son Henri.

On 16 October they went together to the Conciergerie and there, in the vast room known as the 'Hall of the Dead' they found Marie Antoinette reclining in a chair, her head resting against the wall. Two gendarmes guarded her, while nearby stood Bault, the turnkey, and a distressed young woman, Bault's daughter. The gaoler's wife had brought their distinguished prisoner a cup of chocolate and a bread roll, and now, as the two executioners entered, the Queen stood up.

'I had time' [said the Vicomte Charles Desfosses who was present] 'to observe the details of the Queen's appearance and of her dress. She wore a white skirt with a black petticoat under it, a kind of white dressing-jacket, some narrow silk ribbon tied at the wrists, a plain white muslin fichu, and a cap with a bit of black ribbon on it. Her hair was quite white: her face was pale, but there was a touch of red on the cheek-bones; her eyes were bloodshot, and the lashes motionless and stiff.'

Charles-Henri and his son removed their hats deferentially.

'Gentlemen, I am ready,' Marie Antoinette said in a steady voice, and when the executioner explained that some preparations had to be made, she turned slightly to display the back of her neck, where the hair had been cut away in readiness. 'That will do, I think?' she said and, to avoid the indignity of having to be asked, she held out her hands for him to secure.

For spiritual solace and guidance, it had been arranged that she should be accompanied by a priest, and it was then that they were joined by Abbé Lothringer. His presence was not welcomed by the Queen, the priest having taken the oath of fidelity to the Republic; in reply to his murmured request, almost disdainfully she replied, 'You may come with me if you wish.'

The sad entourage, heavily escorted by gendarmes, proceeded to the courtyard where, for the first time, their prisoner saw the waiting tumbril. A fleeting expression of horror passed over her face then, controlling herself, she allowed herself to be assisted into the ramshackle vehicle by Charles-Henri and his son, stepping with some agility over the plank placed crosswise to serve as a bench. She sat down on it, facing the horses, but Charles-Henri persuaded her to turn round and face the other way, so that she would not be able to see the guillotine until the very last moment.

When the party was on board, the ponderous gates leading on to the street were slowly swung open and the cart moved forward, seemingly heading into the great crush of people which filled the entire area, the clamour of abuse and the brandishing of fists causing the horses to rear and whinny in alarm. So imminent was the threat of violence that the two Sansons, mindful of the safety of their royal prisoner, stood up and protected her with their bodies, but throughout the mêlée she sat apparently undisturbed by it all.

The route to the scaffold was as well guarded as at the time of her husband's execution. Cannon had been positioned at all the bridges, squares and road junctions, and 30,000 armed foot soldiers flanked the boulevards in double rows. Behind them the spectators jostled and jeered, but Marie Antoinette had no eyes for them; instead she looked for the numbers of the houses with more than passing curiosity. Anticipating the absence of a priest of her own choosing, she had arranged for a proscribed ecclesiastic, the Abbé du Puget, to be positioned near a certain house in the rue St Honoré on the day of execution, there to give her absolution 'in extremis' as she was driven past. At last she realized that the cart was level with the place she had been so urgently looking for and, at a sign that only she understood from the man who stood on a pile of stones, she bent her head and prayed. Only then did she relax, a faint smile playing around her lips.

As they approached the scaffold site the cart was temporarily halted opposite the Tuileries, the palace in which her two children had been confined. For a moment she swayed, and the Sansons heard her murmur, 'My daughter! My children!' Then the cumbersome cart rumbled on, to halt by the scaffold.

There, impeded by her bound hands, she dismounted, helped by Charles-Henri who, as her feet reached the ground, whispered encouragingly, 'Have courage, Madame!' The Queen looked around, as if surprised to find pity in the heart of the man who was about to decapitate her. She paused for a moment, then answered, 'Thank you, sir, thank you.'

Flanked by the two executioners she moved towards the scaffold and when Henri, the younger executioner, attempted to support her, she exclaimed, 'No; I am, thank Heaven, strong enough to walk that short distance.' As she mounted the steps one of her shoes, of black silk but now shabby and full of holes, slipped from her foot. It was retrieved by a soldier who later sold it to a curio hunter for one gold louis.

On the scaffold confusion reigned, while the vast crowd

seethed and gesticulated around the platform and the drummers beat their staccato rhythm. The abbé, mindful of his religious duty, continued to pray loudly and, impatient to bring merciful death to their victim as quickly as possible, Henri Sanson thrust him aside and bent to the task of securing the Queen to the bascule. Even as he did, Marie Antoinette exclaimed, 'Farewell my children, I am going to join your father.' Next moment the weigh plank was swung horizontally; the lunette clattered into place, and the heavy knife hurtled down, beheading the Queen instantly.

To the cries of '*Vive la République!*' from the crowd, one of the assistant executioners held the head high, the gory trophy then being put, with the corpse, into a coffin of common wood and taken to the cemetery of La Madeleine. There the dresses and undergarments were removed and taken away for disposal and after the body had been covered with quicklime, the coffin was buried near that of her husband the King.

Needless to say, the Paris papers exulted in the death of their enemy. The republican Hébert wrote a virulent article in which he voiced all the corrosive hatred felt by his fellow revolutionists:

> All of you who have been oppressed by our former tyrants, you who mourn a father, a son, or a husband who has died for the Republic, take comfort, for you are avenged. I saw the head of the female Austrian fall into the sack. I wish by God I could describe to you the satisfaction of the *sans-culottes* [the revolutionary mob, so called because they were 'without breeches', wearing instead pantaloons or trousers] when the arch-tigress drove across Paris in the carriage with thirty-six doors [the intervals between the staves that formed the sides of the cart].
>
> She was not drawn by her beautiful white horses with their fine feathers and their grand harness, but by a couple of nags harnessed to Master Sanson's barouche, and they were apparently so glad to contribute to the deliverance of the Republic that they seemed anxious to gallop, in order to reach the fatal spot more quickly. The jade, however, remained bold and insolent to the end. But her legs failed her as she got upon the see-saw to play hot-cockles [the choking

sound made by a victim], in the fear, no doubt, of finding a more terrible punishment before her, after death, than the one she was about to endure. Her accursed head was at last separated from her crane-like neck, and the air was filled with cries of '*Vive la République*'!

It might be of some satisfaction to note that less than six months later Hébert himself fell foul of the political leaders and was condemned to be beheaded. From the moment of leaving the Palais de Justice he was distraught; always well dressed, his clothes were now in disorder. In the tumbril he wept and sobbed, and so cowardly was his behaviour that he disgusted the seventeen victims who were to die with him. He too was roundly jeered and abused by the crowds lining the streets. 'Ah!' cried one bystander. 'You're going to look through the little window [the lunette], and you'll tell us tomorrow in your paper what there is to be seen through it!'

At the scaffold site it was necessary to lift him out of the cart and sit him on the ground, as his legs would no longer support him. Half-fainting, he was nearly dead with fear by the time the executioners bound him to the bascule and released the blade.

Of those who were executed in Paris, the greatest number perished in the Place de la Révolution and more than a thousand of them were buried in the Madeleine cemetery. When the King and Queen were buried, the exact spot was noted by a M. Desclozeaux and his son-in-law, and in 1795 they purchased the graveyard with the pious object of commemorating the spot, and there they planted weeping willows.

The remains lay undisturbed for over two decades, until M. Desclozeaux informed King Louis XVIII. On 18 and 19 January 1815 excavations took place and the remains of the King and Queen, together with shreds of their clothing, even the Queen's garters, were transferred to lead coffins and sealed with the royal insignia.

On 21 January 1815, the twenty-second anniversary of the King's execution, the sad funeral procession took the same route as that taken by the King on his journey to the guillotine. Through streets lined with silent crowds the hearses conveyed the coffins to St Denis, where they were laid to rest in the Bourbon vaults.

In the cemetery itself the Chapelle Expiatoire was built, 'in expiation of the crime by which they had died'. Within it were erected marble statues of the King and Queen with inscriptions in gold around their bases. In the crypt, over the exact spot where the royal pair had been buried so ignominiously, a marble sarcophagus was placed, containing some of the earth and quicklime found adhering to their bones.

The fate of the other members of the royal family was equally tragic. The King's sister, Madame Elizabeth, was accused of conspiracy against the Republic; Charles-Henri attended the trial. Some leniency was afforded her, an armchair being provided, and wild rumours were circulated to the effect that the revolutionary leader Robespierre had hinted that she would be allowed to succeed to the throne if she would marry him. True or not, the Tribunal wasted little time in deciding her fate, and to no one's surprise she was declared guilty. And because a conspiracy consisting of but one person was manifestly impossible, twenty-three others were convicted with her.

At four o'clock on 10 May 1794 the order for her execution was brought to Charles-Henri by his assistant Desmorets. When he went to prepare her, he found her in a room with Richard, the gaoler, whose wife had been telling her how bravely the Queen had died.

While Charles-Henri's son, Henri, and the assistants were preparing the other 'convicts', Madame Elizabeth went with the executioner to the room reserved for women, and there seated herself in a chair so that he could cut her hair away from the nape of her neck. It was auburn, Charles-Henri said, very long and luxuriant; her waist was thick, like the late King's, and her pale face was very full, her cheeks plump.

Accompanied by a bishop, she joined in with him and prayed fervently as she was led to the tumbrils with the others. With the unrivalled sadism that characterized many members of the ruling party, strict orders were given to Charles-Henri that because she had been found guilty of being the leader of the conspiracy, she was to be executed last and so would have to watch the others being beheaded. She therefore remained guarded by the gendarmes at the foot of the scaffold steps, an ordeal which must have lasted at least half an hour. Almost overcome by the sight of the slaughter, and the roar of the mob each time a head was severed, at last her turn came. Trembling slightly she mounted the steps. As quickly as he could, Charles-Henri ensured that she was strapped down on the plank; and the blade fell.

Her remains and those of her fellow sufferers were placed in coffins and taken away on the executioner's carts. Later, after having been covered with quicklime, they were all buried in the cemetery at Mousseaux.

The fate of the King's son and heir, the Dauphin, who should rightly have inherited the throne as King Louis XVII, was no less tragic. After the executions of his parents and close relatives, apart from his sister, he was given into the charge of one Antoine Simon, a cordwainer (shoemaker) employed in the Temple prison, who reportedly encouraged the boy to drink and swear, and also taught him the words of the revolutionary songs, but then shut him up in the squalor and darkness of one of the towers 'his shirt not changed for six months'.

Eventually it was announced by the authorities that the 10-year-old boy had contracted tuberculosis of the bones, and had passed away on 8 June 1795, but this was never confirmed. Comte d'Andigne certainly found the remains of a child in the Temple moat in June 1801, but there was no real proof that they were in fact those of Louis XVII of France. Whether he escaped and earned a meagre living in Holland as a mender of clocks and watches under the name of Naundorff, as was averred by some, or was one of the two dozen pretenders who made their appearance later, is now of scarcely more than academic interest. It is, in any case, one of the most pathetic instances in history of the innocent suffering for the guilty.

There was, however, no dispute at all concerning the fate of Antoine Simon, for Charles-Henri, doubtless with a certain amount of satisfaction, avenged the ill-treatment of the young boy by guillotining his erstwhile tormentor on 28 July 1794.

The sole survivor of the royal carnage was Madame Royale, the King's daughter who, against all the odds, avoided a rendezvous with Charles-Henri and his son by being released in December 1795 in exchange for a large number of French prisoners of war held by the Austrian government.

Hours before she died, Queen Marie Antoinette had written a final, farewell letter to her sister-in-law Princess Elizabeth. This was given to the Prosecutor Fouquier-Tinville but he, rather than risk being accused of showing sympathetic treatment of members of the royal family, passed it to Robespierre. He in turn decided against taking any humane action, and concealed it under his mattress.

There it remained until Robespierre himself was guillotined. During the disposal of his effects the letter was found by M. Curtois, a Deputy of the Convention. He kept it as a souvenir, the intended recipient having already been executed.

Twenty years later he had the temerity to offer it, together with a lock of the dead Queen's hair, to Louis XVIII, in exchange for a pardon for his previous revolutionary activities. It is gratifying to be able to report that Deputy Curtois was promptly arrested, the relics seized, and the thief banished for life to Belgium.

The letter was later shown to Marie Antoinette's daughter, Mme Royale, and on seeing the tear-stained pages written by her mother under such appallingly tragic circumstances, she fainted.

By this time Charles-Henri and his assistants were becoming increasingly affected by the sheer numbers of victims they had to despatch at each execution. As in the case of Madame Elizabeth and her fellow 'conspirators', rarely did the Tribunal assemble in order to try just one accused person; mass trials meant mass executions. This inevitably had a deleterious effect on the executioners who, while operating as quickly as they could on the scaffold, were only too aware of the nervous state of those queuing below, some of whom could be approaching a state of imminent collapse.

It was on 31 October 1793, within days of the execution of the Princess and the others, that the Girondists met the same fate. Under the leadership of Jacques Pierre Brissot de Warville, the political party had fully endorsed the fall of the monarchy and the war against Austria, but eventually came to be regarded as suspiciously moderate by the more powerful and left-wing Jacobins led by Georges Jacques Danton, Camille Desmoulins and Maximilien Marie Isidore de Robespierre. Toleration and reasoned debate being commodities in short supply in the heated political climate of the day, little time was lost in accusing the Girondists of treachery, and twenty-one of their number, all deputies representing various districts of France, were arraigned and tried on a charge of 'conspiring against the unity and indivisibility of the Republic and the safety of the Nation'.

After a semblance of a trial all were found guilty. One, Boileau, threw his hat in the air and cried, 'I die innocent.' Sillery, who was lame, threw away his crutches and declared, 'This day is the finest in my life.' Some appeared downcast but, patriotic even in the face of such dire condemnation, they united in the cry of '*Vive la République* – we are innocent!' At that the President of the Tribunal ordered the gendarmes to conduct the prisoners to the cells, consternation breaking out when it was discovered that one deputy, Dufriche Valaze, had stabbed himself in the heart and lay dying. The ever-malignant Fouquier-Tinville however wasted little time in sympathy; coldly he ordered that when the time came, the corpse was to be placed in the cart with the others, and disposed of with the bodies of his companions after their execution.

That the trial was a mere formality was evidenced by the fact that four days previously, Charles-Henri had been told by Fouquier-Tinville to make arrangements for a large execution in which at least twelve assistants would be required. With considerable effort the executioner managed to recruit this number, and on the fatal day, accompanied by his son Henri and six of the assistants, he went to the Conciergerie.

In the Hall of the Dead they found their victims already assembled, some seated and writing, others talking in groups. By the window, stretched across three stools, lay the corpse of the suicide Valaze.

Nappier, the clerk, called the roll, each of the Girondists

acknowledging his presence, and then the preparation began. The two executioners cut their hair, the assistants binding their hands. While one of the convicts, Ducos, was being attended to, Henri Sanson inadvertently caught some of his hairs in the scissor blades, tearing them out; this induced the deputy, undaunted to the last, to exclaim, 'I hope the edge of your guillotine is sharper than your scissors!'

When all were ready, Charles-Henri gave the signal to leave. Some of the gendarmes had already descended the stairs to the courtyard, and the victims quickly conferred with each other over the order of their departure, but it was Verniaud, one of their leaders, who pointed to Valaze's body, then being placed on a trestle by two of the executioner's assistants, and said, 'He preceded us in death, so he must show us the way.'

The grim procession wended its way to the carts where, in accordance with the orders given by the clerk of the court, they took their places according to their names on the judgement sheet. Five climbed into each of the first two carts, six in the third, four in the fourth, each batch accompanied by an executioner or assistant, and the fifth tumbril brought up the rear, having as its sole passenger the corpse of Valaze.

Although it was an overcast and rainy day, an immense crowd watched as the procession wended its way through the streets. None of the condemned men showed any sign of weakness, some of them singing a chorus of the 'Marseillaise'. On seeing the guillotine as they approached, Ducos, who had joked about the sharpness of the scissor blades, commented with wry humour, 'What a pity it is that the Convention did not decree the unity and indivisibility of our persons!'

After being formed in a line between two rows of gendarmes, the executions began. Deputy Sillery was the first one to be led on to the platform; there, he limped around it slowly and bowed four times to the onlookers. On being told by one of the assistants to hurry, he answered, 'Can't you wait a minute? I wait also, and yet I am in a greater hurry than you are.'

Understandably the executioners did not want the long

queue to wait longer than necessary; the blade came down on Sillery, and then, as the Girondists sang the 'Marseillaise' in chorus, five others met their deaths. Charles-Henri was superintending his assistant Fermin as the man pulled the release rope; his son Henri was in charge of the removal of the bodies, which were thrown,.two at a time, into the baskets waiting behind the guillotine. But when six heads had fallen, the baskets and the bascule were so saturated with blood that Charles-Henri ordered two assistants to throw pails of water over them and sponge them after each decapitation.

This was quickly carried out, and the remaining victims, staunch to the very last, were helped up the steps and duly despatched. The anthem grew fainter, dwindling to a duet, a solo – then finally silence.

It is a tribute to the expertise instilled into the team on the scaffold by Charles-Henri that the awful waiting endured by the condemned was reduced to an absolute minimum, for the execution of the twenty Girondists took just forty-three minutes.

Nor were the headsmen to be short of further practice; from then on not a day passed without executions taking place, the two Sansons, father and son, being continually on the scaffold. The heads of men and women continued to fall, and then on the 6 November 1793, it was the turn of Louis Philippe Joseph, Duke of Orléans, cousin to the late King. Liberal by nature, he opposed his cousin and indeed voted in favour of the monarch's death. His eldest son, Louis Philippe, actively supported France's enemy, Austria, and when, in 1792, all hereditary titles were abolished, the Duke adopted the name 'Philippe Egalité' and became a deputy representing Paris in the Convention.

Despite his allegiance to the Revolution, he had not succeeded in obliterating the memories of his royal birth and immense fortune. Hated by the royalists, his fealty suspected by the republicans, he was a marked man, and after his arrest on 7 April he was imprisoned for six months at Marseilles, together with his two sons. His guilt being a foregone conclusion, he was finally transferred to the Conciergerie in Paris, where he was tried and condemned to death.

By the time Charles-Henri and his team had arrived, Philippe had had a hearty breakfast; a sufficiency of oysters, two cutlets, and the best part of an excellent bottle of claret. As befitted his elegant taste, he wore a green frock-coat over a waistcoat of white cotton fabric, yellow buckskin breeches and high boots. In company with an ex-official named de Laroque, and Pierre Gondier, a stockbroker, he submitted to the necessary preparation. As one of the assistants approached de Laroque, preparatory to cutting his hair, the elderly gentleman took off the wig which covered his bald head and commented drily, 'This renders your formality useless!' A true royalist, he suddenly recognized the duke; flushing with indignation he exclaimed, 'I am no longer sorry to leave life since he who has betrayed my country meets with the punishment he deserves; but, sir, I confess I am much humiliated at having to die on the same scaffold as you!'

The grim procession left at four o'clock, pausing deliberately outside the duke's former palace so that the nobleman could see the words 'national property' written across the front of the building. He looked for a moment at the abode of his ancestors, and then turned scornfully away.

M. de Laroque bade farewell to his companion, ignoring the duke, and then mounted the steps of the scaffold to where Charles-Henri waited. After the knife had fallen, the stockbroker was next, Philippe witnessing the executions without apparent emotion.

Once on the platform he coldly surveyed the people in the crowd who were hissing him. Then, as the executioner raised the blade in readiness, the assistants removed Philippe's coat. On intimating their need to divest him of his boots, he resisted and walked towards the bascule. 'You are losing time,' he said calmly. 'You can take them off at greater leisure when I am dead!'

The guillotine was rarely idle; masons and shoemakers, coopers and labourers, wives and daughters, anyone suspected of disloyalty to the regime, all 'felt the slight breeze on the neck' as the weeks went by. But a much more illustrious victim was soon to be the executioner's guest, in the shape of Marie Jeanne Roland. She had become the enthusiastic supporter and great friend of the leaders of the

Girondists, and was adjudged as guilty of treason as were her former companions. Her husband, Jean-Marie Roland de Platiere, escaped, but she was imprisoned for five months and then, at the age of thirty-nine, condemned to death.

Caustic, witty, contemptuous of mediocrities, she had many admirers but scores of enemies. At her trial, on 8 November 1793, she poured scorn on those who had condemned her political friends, and praised the latter's integrity and patriotism. Her outburst was quelled, not only by the President of the Tribunal but also by the audience's jeers, and eventually she remained disdainfully silent, exclaiming only, when sentence was passed on her; 'You judge me worthy of sharing the fate of the great men you have murdered; I will try to show on the scaffold the fortitude they displayed.'

She was sentenced to be executed immediately after her trial, and so was visited by Charles-Henri. She had very fine black hair, and demurred when he pointed out the need to cut it, explaining that if she retained it, she ran the risk of fearful mutilation should it impede the blade.

Marie seemed touched by his argument and said smilingly, 'Strange that humanity should take refuge in such an unlikely person as you!' And as the raven-black locks fell away, she murmured, 'At least leave me enough for you to hold up my head and show it to the people, if they wish to see it!'

Clad in white, she could hardly have been unobserved by the crowds lining the route, yet they were strangely muted save at one point where shouts of, 'To the guillotine!' were directed at her. Defiantly she replied, 'Soon I'll be there. And those who have sent me will not be long in following me. When they do, you will applaud them as you now applaud me!'

A man, Lamarche, was one of the company in the cart and, observing that his nerve was failing, she comforted him as much as she could. As they stopped by the scaffold, he was on the point of collapse and had to be helped out by an assistant. Seeing this Mme Roland looked at Lamarche with compassion and exclaimed, 'I can only spare you the sight of blood; go first, poor man!'

Fouquier-Tinville, the prosecutor, had already detailed

the order of execution, and Mme Roland had been granted the privilege of dying first. On hearing her intention to allow Lamarche to precede her, Charles-Henri said that it was impossible; that he had orders to the contrary. 'No, no,' replied Mme Roland. 'I am sure you were not ordered to refuse a woman's last request.' Moved by her humane attitude towards her pitiful companion, the executioner had not the courage to persist. Guiding the man up the steps, he attended to his execution. Mme Roland watched the head fall without a shudder; then she too delivered herself into the executioner's hands.

Λ few days later an equally tragic aftermath occurred. Some four leagues from Rouen, slumped against a tree and stiff in death, was found the body of Marie's husband Jean-Marie Roland, who had committed suicide with his cane-sword (swordstick).

Charles-Henri, who felt respect and consideration for members of the opposite sex, was always sickened by having to put women to death, and within the last five months he had had to execute Charlotte Corday, Marie Antoinette, the Princess Elizabeth and Mme Roland, as well as others of lower rank. Yet probably one of the worst days of his many worst days up to then occurred when he had to decapitate Marie Jeanne Gomard de Vaubernier, Comtesse du Barry, the woman he never denied having loved. Rashly she had returned from England after the outbreak of the Revolution in the mistaken belief that she would be safe but, despite claiming that she had been born the daughter of a priest and a dressmaker and so was not an aristocrat, she was charged by the Tribunal that as a royal mistress she had squandered the treasures of the State and had worn mourning for the late king.

In his diary for that day (6 December 1793) he described the harrowing scenes in heartfelt detail:

Madame du Barry was sentenced to death last night and executed this morning. We arrived at the Hall of Justice punctually but had to wait as the convict [du Barry] was with the judges who were taking down her confession. Then she was brought in; her legs could hardly carry her. It was some

Madame du Barry

twenty years since I had seen her, and I could hardly have known her. Her features had become coarse. When she saw me she shrieked, covered her eyes with her hands, and sank down on her knees, crying, 'Do not kill me!'

She rose to her feet again; 'Where are the judges?' she exclaimed. 'I have not confessed everything; I want to see them.' The judge and his clerk were sent for, and she said she had concealed several objects of value in her country house, but she broke down and sobbed at every word. The clerk kept saying, 'Is that all?' and tried to make her sign the confession, but she pushed the paper away, saying that she had something more to add. She perhaps thought that, in reason of the immense wealth she was giving up, she might be reprieved.

At last the judge said that she must submit to the court's decision and make up by her courage for the ignominy of her past life as a member of the royal court. One of my assistants approached and attempted to cut her hair, but she resisted, and the other assistants had great difficulty in binding her hands. She at last submitted, but she cried as I never saw a woman cry before.

Vast crowds had assembled, and many cries were raised, but her shrieks were louder than any. She exclaimed, 'Good citizens, free me! I am innocent; I am of the people, good citizens do not let them kill me!' No one moved, but men and women hung their heads and silence prevailed at last.

Du Barry was so faint that my son Henri had to support her. She often spoke to me, begging for mercy. I was more moved than anyone, for this unfortunate woman reminded me of my younger days, of the time when I knew her.... When she saw the guillotine she became overwrought and struggled with my assistants and tried to bite them. She was very strong, and three minutes elapsed before they could carry her up on to the platform. She was frightful to look at, and to the very last moment she struggled.

Efficient and professional as he may have appeared on the scaffold, nevertheless as the weeks and months went by, the entries in his diary show the strain which was being imposed upon him; reveal too the revulsion he felt at this massacre of his fellow human beings.

Citoyenne St Amaranthe and her daughter arrested, with their servants and friends. One friend was an actress Maria Grandmaison, and her servant Marie Nicole Bouchard. The latter was only eighteen years old and she was so thin and delicate that she did not appear to be more than fourteen.

When the poor little girl held out her hands to my assistant Lariviere, he turned to my chief assistant, Desmorets, and exclaimed, 'Surely this is a joke?' Desmorets shrugged his shoulders, and it was the little one who, smiling through her tears, answered, 'No, sir, it is serious.' Whereupon Lariviere threw down the cords and exclaimed, 'Let someone else bind her. It is not my profession to execute children!'

She was calm and resigned. There was a delay in starting, and little Nicole sat down at her mistress's feet and tried to console her. I really believe that if she had begged for her life, more than one would have freed her and offered to take her place. What we felt, the people felt also. The crowd was very large, owing to the number being executed. The hundreds of gendarmes who escorted us, and the cannon which followed in the rear, had induced all Parisians to come out. Five or six pretty women were in the first cart, and their fate excited pity; but when poor little Nicole Bouchard was seen, there was an explosion of indignation. Cries of 'No children!' rose numerous and loud.

In the Faubourg St Antoine I could see women weeping. I was almost overpowered by this scene. I had looked at Nicole Bouchard at the Conciergerie prison and her eyes, to my way of thinking, pleaded with me not to kill her. And yet she is dead now. She was the ninth to climb the steps. When she passed before me I had to struggle with a sudden temptation which whispered in my ear, 'Smash up the guillotine, and do not allow this child to die!'

My assistants pushed her towards the knife. I turned away; my legs trembled and I felt sick. It was Martin [his brother] who had charge of this execution. He said to me, 'You are unwell. Go home, and trust me for the rest of the executions.'

I did not answer, and left the scaffold. I was in a fever, and so scared that at the corner of the rue Saint Onge, when a woman stopped me and begged, I thought the little girl was before me.

This morning I had to take two carts from the Conciergerie to the scaffold. Five convicts in one cart, four in the other. In this number I saw a mother and her son, we had to use force to separate them. When the mother saw her child's hair being cut off in readiness, her shrieks were so heart-rending that we could hardly bear to hear them. It was too much for me; Henri [his son] took the first cart and I went in the other one, but on the way, despite the noise from the crowd, I could hear the woman groaning and weeping. The convicts in my cart turned away so as not to see her. The son kept saying that he was glad to die with his mother; she suffered first, and on the platform she said to me, 'I am sure he is to be reprieved.' I think she had the idea that her son had been brought with her merely to frighten her – I thought it of no use to contradict her.

Today we executed Antoine de Tontel, lieutenant colonel, and Clement Laverdy, formerly superintendent of finances, convicted of having contributed to famine by throwing corn into a pond. A nasty task. The first convict was seventy-two years old, the other seventy. Both died with courage.

Executed twenty-three men and four women today. One of the men had a dog which was much attached to its master. It followed him to prison and remained at the door till the carts came out of the yard. On recognizing its master it barked with joy and followed us all the way. When we got to the scaffold the dog would not leave its master and ran up on to the platform. One of my men threw it down but it rushed back up the steps and began to howl dismally; whereupon a gendarme pinned it with his bayonet. Strange to say, the people, who can stand and see a human being murdered, took the dog's part. Stones were aimed at the gendarme and he narrowly escaped with his life. A workman took up the dog and carried it away.

This morning, executed one of the great lords of the defunct monarchy, the Duc du Chatelet. In the night he had attempted to destroy himself; having neither knife nor dagger, he tried to kill himself with a sharp piece of glass, but the glass broke and only made a slight wound. Then thinking that he could die by losing all his blood, he cut his breast several times with the pieces, but only succeeded in weakening himself so much that his legs would not carry him. Nevertheless his heart was firm. I proposed in the cart to bind his wounds and therefore prevent the blood from flowing, but he answered, 'Never mind; it's only saving you work!'

Last month, at the bidding of the Commune [the committee that governed Paris during the Terror] I had been ordered to remove the blood which had oozed through the boards of the scaffold. A pit had been made which had been covered with trellis work to keep the dogs out, but the blood dried too quickly and could not be absorbed by the earth, causing an unbearable smell to come from the pit. And anyway the soil that surrounded the scaffold was always soaked with blood, to such a point that the footsteps of those who crossed the square could be traced to a great distance. Last night I instructed my assistants to dig the pit deeper.

The summer of 1794 was particularly hot in France. In July the heat was excessive; at the coolest time of the night the thermometer was never lower than sixteen or eighteen degrees. Both men and animals were overwhelmed by the heat, and died; the vegetables in gardens and fields were burnt or devoured by the caterpillars that were hatched out by the heat. Furniture and woodwork cracked, doors and windows became warped. The prevailing winds were from the north and east, and the sky was nearly always cloudless. The unhygienic effect of such temperatures on the conditions on – and beneath – the scaffolds can well be imagined. Orders were despatched to all towns insisting that executioners clean their guillotines thoroughly after use by throwing water over them and brushing them down. They were also to collect the blood in a barrel (just how, was not specified), this to be emptied immediately after each execution.

Sanson's diary continued:

Another General of our Army died today on the guillotine. Borin had been sentenced yesterday. When I went for him he was in the head turn-key's room and was eating oysters with much appetite. On seeing me he said, 'Allow me to eat this last dozen of oysters!' I answered that I was at his orders, which made him laugh and say, 'No, *morbleu*! It's just the other way round – I am at yours!' He finished the repast with wonderful tranquillity, joking with me and saying that he should arrive in the other world in time to wish a happy new year to his friends. He was cool to the end.

Seventeen persons were sentenced to death yesterday; I executed them this morning. This execution was one of the most lamentable in which I ever took part. The women were in a majority and several had their children in the carts. All were convicted of conspiracy against liberty. The sight was affecting in the extreme, for the women moaned and cried.

When the King of Prussia visited Verdun last year, some of the inhabitants presented him with the keys of the town. The wives and daughters of the burghers offered him flowers, and were present at a ball given in the enemy's honour by the royalist muncipality and the women danced with Prussian officers. The ringleaders have been tried for this crime by the Revolutionary Tribunal and thirty-four, men and women, were sentenced to death. Had to execute them all today, and a terrible day's work it was.

Today we executed some ladies of quality, and they showed much tranquillity. With them was Jean-Joseph Payen, an erstwhile tenant farmer of the Marquise de Marboeuf, one of the ladies in the cart. Observing his trembling hands she exhorted him to die courageously, saying, 'After all, my dear fellow, it's just the same whether we die today or in twenty years time.' 'If it's just the same,' replied Payen, who was not at all resigned to his fate, 'I would rather die in twenty years!'

A very unfortunate accident happened today. All but one convict had been executed, and as he, a peasant named Laroque, was being strapped to the bascule, my son Henri, who was depositing the corpses in the baskets, called to me and I went across to him. Lariviere, one of the assistants, forgot to raise the blade after the last execution, so that when the bascule, with Laroque secured to it, was swung horizontal, his face struck the side of the blade, which was bloody. He uttered a terrible shriek and trembled like a leaf. The mob hissed us and threw stones at us. In the evening Prosecutor Fouquier severely reprimanded me. I deserved his blame, for I should have been in my usual place. The Prosecutor saw that I was very sorry, and dismissed me with more kindness than I expected.

Since the guillotine is now the order of the day, inventors are always thinking of modifying it. Over twenty suggestions have been presented to the revolutionary committee, but they are so absurd that only one was worthy of consideration. The plan consists of a trap opening near the weigh plank, into which the headless body falls, as a method of reducing the accumulation of bodies on the scaffold. An experiment was made but it did not succeed, the two bags of sand which were used having failed to enter the trap. When asked for my opinion I said that the proposed alteration was full of danger; that if the trap did not close better than it opened, the executioners or the victims might fall through it with the corpses. The proposal was shelved.

(Later, some individual provinces did modify their own guillotines in various ways, one scaffold incorporating a hole beneath the device into which the bodies fell, probably into a large container, for subsequent removal to the cemetery. It would also be logical to assume that the heads, after being displayed to the crowd, would also be tossed into the hole.)

This morning I received a visit of a maniac, who asked me to look at a projected guillotine with three knives, which he had invented. He really amused me. His pride and his hatred against aristocrats were really very comical. His discovery, he said, would consolidate the Republic. He left me, saying that he would bring it to the attention of the authorities.

A terrible day's work today. The Tribunal passed sixteen sentences of death. All the convicts were natives of La Nievre who had taken part in an insurrection. The execution lasted thirty-two minutes.

There was a time when the women were, as a rule, stronger and pluckier than the men. Not so now. They weep, tremble and beg for mercy. We have had a fearful day. The Faubourg St Antoine cannot forget it. My carts contained twenty-three women of different ages and social standing. Each turn of the wheels was marked by a sob. Their shrieks were awful to hear. The crowd dispersed and we made our way along deserted streets. My men were more than usually dark and sullen. One of them said, 'They compel us to disgrace the scaffold.' I was not left to suffer alone today.

Days follow each other and are alike. Twenty-one more victims today. There are some people who say that one gets used to the blood; this is not true, when the blood is human blood. I do not speak of myself, but of my assistants, whom I observe. Two of them have been with me for the last twelve years, four others were butchers' boys; there are at least two of them who are not worth a rope to hang them with, and yet there is not one who is not moved after a wholesale execution. The public perceives nothing, but often I see their legs tremble. When everything is finished, and they see only corpses around them on the scaffold, they look astonished and uneasy. If such is their impression, what must be that of the people?

Formerly when I used to enter the prison, my appearance frightened the boldest; now among the prisoners I meet in the corridors and the cells, not one of them seems to think that tomorrow, perhaps, I shall call for him. There are some smiles when I enter. These smiles have a singular effect on me. Experience has made me callous, and I can almost bear the horror with which we executioners are regarded; but to get used to those people who almost say, 'Thank you' when they are led to the guillotine, is more difficult. My hand could not have remained firm if it had still to carry out the sentences under the older regime [i.e. to swing the sword]. Judges, jurors, prisoners, all seem as if they were taking part in a delirium of death. When shall all this end?

One last, utterly revealing entry, exposes the traumatic effects on Charles-Henri of the continued slaughter:

A terrible day's work! The guillotine devoured fifty-four victims. My strength is at an end, and I almost fainted away. A caricature has been shown to me in which I am represented guillotining myself in the middle of a heath covered with headless bodies and bodiless heads, because there is no one left to decapitate. I do not boast of extraordinary squeamishness; I have seen too much blood in my life not to be callous. If what I feel is not pity, it must be a derangement of the nerves. Perhaps I am being punished by the Almighty for my cowardly obedience to mock justice.

For some time now I have been troubled with terrible visions. I am taken with fever as soon as I enter the Conciergerie; it is like fire flowing under my skin. Abstemious as I am, it seems to me as if I am intoxicated – the people who are around me, the furniture, the walls, dance and whirl around me, and my ears are full of strange noises. My hands tremble, and tremble so much that I have been compelled to give up cutting the hair of the doomed prisoners. They are before me, weeping and praying, and I cannot convince myself of the reality of what is going on. I lead them to death, but I cannot believe that they are going to die. It is like a dream which I strive to dispel. I follow the preparations for the tragedy, and I have no idea what is to occur next, and I perform my duties with the mechanical regularity of a robot.

Then comes the thump of the knife, which reminds me of the horrible reality. I cannot hear it now without a shudder. A kind of rage then takes possession of me. Forgetting that I ought to blame myself more than others, I abuse the gendarmes who, sabres in hand, have escorted the prisoners; I abuse the people who look on without raising a finger in their defence; I even abuse the sun which lightens all this. At length I leave the scaffold, disposed to weep, although I cannot find a tear. And when I get home and sit down to dinner, I see spots of blood on the tablecloth.

As has been said before, he could have resigned, even at the cost of his own life. Yet it is evident from his own words that, such was the sympathy he felt for his victims, he was prepared to endure his own sufferings for as long as he could, in order to provide some small but merciful relief for them in their final, terrible moments.

This humane attitude of Charles-Henri's was commented on by the Abbé Carrishon who, secretly attending an execution for the purpose of giving a last blessing to three of his flock, Madame de Marechal de Noailles, Madame la Duchesse d'Ayen, and her daughter the Vicomtesse, said

> The tumbrils drew up, the scaffold appeared; I shivered. It was at once surrounded by the horsemen and foot soldiers. Behind them were numerous spectators in a circle. Most of them were laughing and enjoying the heartrending sight.
>
> I perceived Sanson, the chief executioner and his two assistants, and it must be admitted that, whether from an underlying feeling of humanity or from habit, the torture was singularly alleviated by their promptitude, and they took care to place all the victims with their backs to the scaffold in order that they should be unable to see anything.
>
> I felt rather kindly towards them for this, and also for the decorous manner and unchanging gravity they maintained, without any mocking or insulting treatment of the victims.

Most crowds looked on executions as a source of entertainment, but the effect on spectators not possessing the revolutionary lust for blood was traumatic. An historian, Charles Maurice, born in 1782, was only a small boy when, one day, he watched the tumbrils pass by. Later he gave a heart-rending account of an episode which had imprinted itself on his very soul, writing:

> How did it happen that I was there, young as I was? It is one of those things that I am reduced to classing among the enigmas of my life. However it may have been, I saw it, that tomb on wheels. It was filled with unfortunate creatures going to their death, all men.
>
> One of them – I could portray his face with all its anguish before he began to speak, and his resignation as soon as he had uttered the words – called out, 'Is there anyone here who will go to number sixteen in the Rue de la Vielle-Draperie?'
>
> 'I will go,' I answered, prompted by a movement of pity I can still feel, though I was under the eyes of the crowd, who

dared not show their approval. 'Thank you, my boy,' he went on. 'Go and tell my wife and children that I die loving them, and that they must console each other.'

'I will go this minute,' I said, rushing off in the direction that was pointed out to me; and I went, and fulfilled my promise; child that I was, deeply moved but understanding neither the causes of the drama I had witnessed, nor the difficulty and magnitude of the task I had undertaken to play.

Even worse than for a bystander must have been the effect on relatives themselves. Even if they knew that their loved ones had been arrested and condemned to death – which was not always the case – they were never told where the remains were buried.

One elderly lady, a lace-maker named Mme Paris, lost two members of her own family in this cruel manner, and her pitiful account encapsulates all the horror experienced by those whose nearest and dearest had been slaughtered in the name of the Revolution.

My father André [she said] was an infirm old man who had served as groom and coach-driver to the Duc de Brissac for thirty years; my brother François was employed at the headquarters of the National Guard. François was very steady and economical and he supported us all by his work, for the downfall of the Duc and his family had deprived my father of a pension, and as for me, I was entirely without work, since no one wore any lace at the time of the Terror.

One day my brother did not return home at the usual hour; I went out in search of him, but when I came back I found the house deserted; my father, who was almost unable to walk, had been taken off to prison in my absence. I then found out that my brother had been in the same prison since the morning.

I never heard what they were charged with, nor could I obtain leave to be imprisoned with them, nor even to embrace them. I never saw them again except in the cart that took them to their deaths. A man who saw me watching the procession recognized me and wanted to take me away with him, for pity; and when I refused to go, he went away himself, weeping.

I saw my father and my brother guillotined, and if I did not die on the spot it was because God sustained me. I did not even fall down, but remained standing where I was, stammering some prayers, but quite mechanically, without hearing or seeing anything.

When I came to my senses the square was already nearly deserted, and the spectators were dispersing in every direction. The bloodstained tumbrils, in which the bodies of the poor victims had been placed, were setting out on the road to the country, surrounded by gendarmes. I did not know where they were going, but although it was all I could do to walk, I followed them. They drew up at the cemetery at Picpus; it was nearly night, but I saw the spot where the unfortunate people who had just been guillotined were buried all together. Since that day I have been there often, it is my Sunday walk.

That particular cemetery was later closed and sold to a local resident, who secretly contacted a fugitive priest to consecrate it. The owner subsequently disposed of it to the Princess of Hohenzollern, whose brother, the Prince of Salm-Kilburg, guillotined with fifty-two others on 22 July 1794, had been interred there.

The adjoining plot of ground, which contained an extensive trench used also as a common grave, was owned by Mme de Montagu and Mme de Lafayette, and in time the two cemeteries were made one. A subscription list of the relatives of those buried there was formed, and the Picpus cemetery became a place of worship and remembrance. A large chapel was erected, containing marble tablets on which were inscribed the names of the 1,307 victims buried there. The surrounding area remained untouched, poplars and willows overshadowing the trench-tomb, which was marked by a cross of iron.

The memory of those guillotined is perpetuated by the nuns of the nearby convent who offer prayers in the chapel, and each year a solemn service is held there. Afterwards a formal procession of descendants of the dead, led by the clergy, visits the burial ground, to pray in the sacred enclosure known as the Field of Martyrs.

Lest it be thought that such tragedies were confined to

Paris, it should be remembered that, after models of guillotines had been distributed to the provincial councils to enable them to train potential executioners or update the current office holders, full-size versions were issued and used. It has been estimated that over twenty thousand people met their deaths beneath their blades and were buried in makeshift trenches similar to those in the cemeteries of Picpus and La Madeleine.

By the end of 1793 Charles-Henri must have thought that the time had come when he could perhaps dismantle the guillotine and return it to his store-room, or at least employ it for use solely on genuine criminals. Most of the royals and thousands of aristocrats and dissenters had been executed; the opposition party, the Girondists, had been disposed of in similar fashion, leaving the reins of power in the hands of the extremists led by their founders Georges Jacques Danton, Simplice Camille Benoist Desmoulins and Maximilien Marie Isidore de Robespierre. Surely now the violence could cease, and the revolutionary government would concentrate on stabilizing the country and uniting its people?

Those at least were the measures urged by some of the leaders, for the wars and the years of horror and deprivation had taken their toll on the state of the nation. Inflation had rocketed, and famine threatened, bringing a flourishing black market in such commodities as eggs, butter, grain, sugar, salt, even soap and cooking oil.

The two most closely involved with such a temperate policy were Danton and Desmoulins. Danton, a veritable giant of a man with beetling black brows and a voice of thunderous power, had dominated the Revolution from its very inception, using his forceful personality to override all opposition and reshape France's social patterns in accordance with his ideals. He had voted for the death of the King and the annihilation of the upper classes, and had crushed the Girondists. Personifying the very Terror itself, he and Desmoulins had been the heroes of the hour following the fall of the Bastille. Danton had assumed the post of Minister of Justice, Desmoulins becoming his Secretary. Now however, both of them advocated clemency; it was time to reduce the powers of the ruthless Tribunal, time for the healing of old wounds. Desmoulins, not afraid at one time of saying that it was necessary to embrace liberty on a heap of dead bodies, now asked whether, among so many committees with powers of arrest and punishment, there ought not to be a Committee of Mercy.

But not even the strength of Danton's personality was enough to protect him from the machinations of revolutionary politics. Robespierre and his Committee of Public Safety were determined to continue the policy of violence and ferocity. Anyone not toeing the party line, those engaging in subterfuge or treachery, were to be eliminated. One Committee order instructed a Citizen Demaillot to proceed to Orléans as their secret agent, there to seek out conspirators and enemies of the Revolution. He was to take note of the conduct of officials and denounce them to the Committee. 'He will live as a private individual,' the Order continued, 'and will exercise no authority, but will confine himself to the surveillance entrusted to him and will write daily to the Committee.'

It was in this atmosphere of dread and distrust that, on 30 March 1794 Danton, Desmoulins and fourteen others of like sentiment, were arrested and taken to prison. There, shocked and disbelieving, some tried to formulate a defence; others grew sullen and resigned. Lucile Desmoulins, Camille's 23-year-old wife, visited the adjoining gardens in the hope that her husband could catch sight of her and their baby son Horace, and so Camille spent much of his time at the barred windows.

On 2 April they were brought before the Tribunal and were interrogated by the Public Prosecutor Fouquier-Tinville who, ironically enough, was Desmoulins's cousin and had in fact been appointed to his present position by his relative whilst Secretary of Justice! Ignoring the relationship the Prosecutor demanded to know his cousin's name and age. Desmoulins replied, 'Thirty-three,' reportedly adding, 'The same age as the *sans-culotte* Jesus – a critical age for any patriot!'

His colleague General Westerman commented bitterly, 'I was a soldier at sixteen. I have seven wounds in front, but none in the back – till now.' However, few tears need be shed on his behalf; when he was instrumental in the defeat of the 1793 insurrection in the Vendée region of France, in which thousands of people were guillotined, shot, sabred or drowned, he wrote to the Ministry of Public Safety in Paris:

> There is no longer a Vendée. She is dead under our free sword with her women and children. I have just buried her in the marshes and woods of Savenay in obedience to the orders you gave me. I have crushed the children under the feet of the horses and massacred the women, who will breed no more brigands. I have not to reproach myself with a prisoner, for I have exterminated all of them. The roads are strewn with corpses. There are so many in several places that they form pyramids. The shooting by firing squads at Savenay goes on without ceasing, because every minute brigands arrive who pretend to surrender themselves as prisoners. We take no prisoners. If we did it would be necessary to give them the bread of liberty, and pity is not revolutionary.

General Westerman could hardly complain, therefore, if pity was equally denied him.

Another of Danton's colleagues, Lacroix, exclaimed prophetically 'I think we had better make ready to meet Sanson.' Danton himself, the man who had instituted the Tribunal, electrified those watching with his eloquence. But it was to no avail; all were sentenced to death.

Among those who daily thronged the public galleries during the trial was Charles-Henri. He attended every sitting of the Tribunal, and in the evenings would relate the proceedings to Marie-Anne and Henri. After the sentence, he was sent for by Fouquier-Tinville and his officials, to receive his orders. The prisoners might resist, might incite the crowd, he was told, so was warned that his horses should go at a trot. Speed on the scaffold was also essential; the sooner the 'ruffians' died, the prosecutor said, the better.

After the preparations – Sanson himself attending to Danton's hair 'which was thick and hard like a mane' – they were loaded into the carts and, under heavy escort, moved off. Camille Desmoulins, still barely able to accept his fate, shouted, 'Do you not recognize me? The Bastille fell at my bidding! Come to my help, republicans – do not let them murder us!' Such were his struggles that Sanson had to threaten to tie him to the side of the tumbril, and Danton, realizing that rescue was out of the question, growled, 'Be quiet! Do not hope to soften this vile rabble!'

En route the carts passed Robespierre's house and although the despot was not in sight, Danton roared, 'You shall appear in this cart in your turn, Robespierre, and the soul of Danton will howl with joy!'

At the scaffold the erstwhile leader turned to Charles-Henri, his resolute manner failing slightly as he said, 'Have you not a wife and children?' Sanson replied that he had, whereupon Danton murmured, 'So have I; I was thinking of them,' adding, 'My wife, I shall not then see you again! My child, I shall never see you!' (Mme Danton was pregnant at the time.)

Eight of the Jacobins died first, Camille Desmoulins then being led up the steps. As a last favour he asked the executioner to take a lock of his hair to his mother-in-law (he had learned that his wife Lucile had been arrested) and then without hesitation walked to the bascule, followed by the others.

Danton had looked on with almost unbelievable composure while his friends were being executed. Charles-Henri described how

> Not a muscle of his face moved. He seemed to defy not only the fear of death, but death itself. The weigh plank was hardly lowered and its occupant, Sechelles, executed, when he advanced. I advised him to turn round while the body was being removed. He shrugged his shoulders contemptuously. 'Do not forget to show my head to the mob; they have not often seen one like it!' he exclaimed.

The next day Charles-Henri fulfilled his promise to Desmoulins. At the house, 17 rue des Arcs, he handed the packet containing the lock of hair to a servant, understandably not wishing to identify himself as the man who had decapitated Camille, but on turning away he was called back by M. Duplessis, Camille's father-in-law. Having little option, the executioner followed his host into the house, his heart sinking as he saw a baby in a cradle.

'It is his son,' Duplessis said, continuing, 'You were

there? You saw him? He died a brave man? Like a republican?' Charles-Henri, appalled at his own predicament, could only answer that Camille's last words had been for those he loved. Worse was to follow, for Duplessis turned pale and exclaimed, 'And my poor daughter, my Lucile! Will they kill her, as they killed him?' Next moment an elderly lady entered the room, to throw herself into the arms of M. Duplessis, and Charles-Henri wished he was anywhere else in the world than in that room, for she cried pitifully, 'Lucile is lost! She is to appear before the Tribunal in three days time!' Somehow the executioner managed to leave the house, his emotions in turmoil, needing the solicitude of Marie-Anne to steady his nerves sufficiently for him to resume his work.

On 8 April he went to collect Lucile Desmoulins for her last journey. During her trial it was thought that she was deranged, such was her behaviour, and it was even hoped that she might be reprieved on account of her obviously unhinged mind. But she recovered somewhat in court and was condemned to death, together with others, including the wife of Hébert, who had died so cowardly some months before.

In the cart Charles-Henri was intensely moved by her courage. When he tried to reassure her, she exclaimed, 'Look at me, and say whether my face is that of a woman who needs consolation. My only wish, since Camille's death, has been to join him. If I did not detest those who have condemned me, because they murdered the best and most honest of men, I would bless them for the boon they now confer on me.' At the scaffold she mounted the steps without hesitation, and met her death without flinching. All Charles-Henri could do in mitigation was to send a lock of her hair to her father and mother, but this time employing a messenger.

Robespierre and his supporters now seemed to be unopposed in the Convention and the mass executions continued unabated. Among them was that of the Abbé de Salignac-Fenelon, an elderly cleric who had cared for and comforted the multitude of poverty-stricken boys who scraped a mean living by sweeping the city's chimneys. The scaffold site was surrounded by these diminutive members of his flock, and the abbé asked Sanson whether his hands might be freed so that he could bless them for the last time. The executioner, his emotions touched, immediately acceded, stepping back and bowing his head, as indeed did many of the crowd, upon the abbé making the sign of the cross. Similar reverence was shown some days later when sixteen Carmelite nuns were to be decapitated. Charles-Henri, horrified at his iniquitous task and in defiance of his orders, immediately permitted them to sing a hymn and genuflect to their Mother Superior before bowing to the blade.

Public reactions to these atrocities were however beginning to make themselves shown, one being the attempted assassination of the leader. As in the case of Charlotte Corday, again a woman was involved, this time a 20-year-old paper-dealer's daughter named Cecile Renaud. She had aroused the suspicions of those who guarded Robespierre by her insistence on speaking with him, and in a basket which she had left in a nearby shop were found female clothing and two knives. When questioned she said that she would need the clothes in the prison to which she would surely be sent before being guillotined. And so she was, dying on Charles-Henri's scaffold, together with her father and all her relatives.

Another attempt, this time on the life of Representative Collot, was made by a man named Amiral. Waiting on the stairs, Amiral fired his pistol but there was only a flash in the pan and nothing more (hence the saying). Again he fired but once more the flint failed to ignite the gunpowder. Amiral, captured and tried, also kept a rendezvous with the executioner.

Blame for such an attempt was laid at the door of the English, with whom the country was at war. As a result the Convention passed a decree which enacted that no English soldiers or their Hanoverian allies were to be taken prisoner. The implication of this, that those captured would be summarily shot, was not lost on Charles-Henri, who promptly conjectured the fate of captured French soldiers!

Not all victims were undeserving of their fate, of course. One such was Euloge Schneider, a former priest who had managed to obtain for himself a lucrative post as prosecutor of the Strasburg Revolutionary Tribunal. Too powerful a man to cross, he travelled around Alsace with his tribunal, his guillotine and the Strasburg executioner, obliging inhabitants to illuminate their houses when he passed, levying contributions, passing capital sentences and virtually plundering whatever took his fancy.

Nor did he neglect his close friends, one of whom, Tunck, expressed a wish to marry. So Schneider ordered a parade of all the girls in the town of Barr and invited his friend to choose for himself. To crown his audacity he ordered the executioner to collect money around the scaffold as a present for bride and groom.

Shortly after, Schneider, rather than deprive himself of feminine company, sent a message to a resident of Barr at one o'clock in the morning, ordering him to bring his attractive young daughter to his house. Not daring to refuse, the man obeyed, and on the following day Schneider returned to Strasburg with the girl, in a carriage drawn by six horses.

But nemesis, in the shape of a high-ranking official of the Revolution, had just arrived in the city and on hearing of the man's dictatorial exploits, ordered his immediate arrest. Schneider was exhibited for three hours on his own guillotine, then sent under escort to Paris for trial.

Guilty, he was passed over to Charles-Henri, who wrote in his diary:

> This terrible Schneider has been very humble and small in my hands. He was a broad-shouldered, thick-necked man, well knit and as strong as a bull; his face was sinister and altogether repulsive. He tried to joke, and spoke jocularly of the thickness of his neck, but he could not go on. Tears came to his eyes and a tremor shot through his frame. On the Place de la Révolution he called me 'Sir, sir, sir!' not knowing what he was saying as he went under the knife.

Rarely being able to escape from his scaffold duties, Sanson welcomed the chance one day, when his assistant Martin offered to stand in for him, to take his young nieces out into the country. It was then that, by sheer coincidence, he met the great Robespierre himself. So unusual was it for members of the public to see the great leader except at a distance, that Charles-Henri's description of the encounter makes fascinating reading.

> We went through Clichy and into the countryside. The little girls romped in the fields and I ran about with them, but my old legs soon had enough of this, and I sat down by the side of the road.
>
> Presently I saw a citizen, accompanied by a black and white dog, come along. He looked at the children, who were trying to reach some wild roses in the hedge, and obligingly came to their help. He picked the flowers and divided them among the two little girls. I saw the little ones kiss the citizen.
>
> They came up to me, talking, and it was then that I recognized the stranger. He wore a dark blue coat, yellow breeches and a white waistcoat. His hair was powdered and carefully combed, and he held his hat in his hand. His gait was stiff, his head was slightly thrown backwards, and his face wore a look of gaiety which surprised me.
>
> Citizen Robespierre asked me if the children were mine. I replied that they were my nieces, and he congratulated me on their beauty. Mary made a small nosegay and offered it to him; he took it and stuck it in his buttonhole. He then asked her name so as, he said, to remember her when the flowers faded. The poor child not only gave her Christian name, but added her surname; whereupon Robespierre's face instantly changed. He said to me in a dry and haughty voice, 'You are ...?' I bowed. For a few seconds he was thoughtful; he was evidently struggling against a repulsion which he could not master. At length he bent down, kissed the children very tenderly, called his dog, and went away without looking at me.

Just as with the executioner's meetings with Louis XVI, so it was not long before he met Robespierre again, but this time on the scaffold. The Tribunal's sweeping powers were now such that no deputy in the Convention was immune from sudden arrest and execution. The slightest dissent by any member brought instant and fatal retribution. So factions were formed, secret meetings held, all conspiring against the man who now threatened their very lives.

Robespierre, sensing their opposition, accused them of plotting his downfall, and appealed to their loyalty and patriotism, but it was too late. Orders went out for his arrest, together with his brother Augustin, his henchmen St Just, Couthon, Lebas, Henriot, Payan and Dumas, and other supporters. Deputy Couthon was partially paralysed, the result of a youthful escapade when the unexpected return of a husband required him to take refuge down a well shaft. Transported everywhere in a chair, his habit of carrying his little pet dog with him deceived those who met him into thinking he was gentle and kind. Disillusionment would rapidly follow, as the insurgents of Lyons found out when he crushed their rebellion; standing on high ground he watched with obvious satisfaction the fifty or so executions he had ordered each day.

Not content with that, he had most of the finest houses, those owned by aristocrats, demolished, after he had been carried through the streets and indicated which residences were doomed by striking their front doors with a little silver hammer he carried and saying, 'The Law strikes thee.' Whereupon the masons and labourers would arrive and, with crowbars and wedges, would reduce the buildings to rubble and ruin.

At about the same time as Robespierre and his cohorts were arrested, forty-five victims had been sentenced to death by the Tribunal. Among them was Lieutenant-General Loiserolles whose son was in Saint Lazare prison awaiting execution. On hearing of the death-list the soldier had gone to the prison and, the youth being asleep, he sacrificed himself by answering his son's name when the roll was called and joined the others in the tumbril.

When news of the political upheaval filtered through, the condemned men and women were overjoyed at the prospect of their sentences being overturned, of being freed to return to their families. Charles-Henri was equally hopeful of perhaps being able to save his prisoners from the scaffold; he therefore determined to try to gain time by requesting a twenty-four hour postponement of the executions. Accordingly he went in search of the Public Prosecutor and eventually ran him to ground dining with friends. But his hopes were dashed when Fouquier-Tinville waved his plea away with a gesture of impatience. 'This has nothing to do with us' he exclaimed. 'Sentence has been passed; nothing can impede its immediate execution.'

Crestfallen, Sanson returned to the Conciergerie, where the prisoners had already been prepared for the scaffold by his assistants. Some were weeping, others praying, but Charles-Henri had no option but to load them into the waiting carts. However he was still determined to risk all in order to delay events, and so he said to his assistant Lariviere, 'We shall not go further than the Bastille; the people are so tired of the slaughter that they may free our prisoners and prevent the executions. So much the better!'

When they reached the Place de la Bastille they encountered a large crowd, and a woman in one cart shouted hysterically, 'Mercy, citizens! We are not enemies of the people! Save us, save us!' This was a signal for a chorus of prayers and sobs from her agitated companions, and Sanson's assistants would not have resisted, had the crowd made a concerted attempt to free their prisoners. But other than an isolated cry of 'Mercy!' and 'No guillotine!', the people surrounding the carts just looked on helplessly, albeit with expressions of compassion on their faces. Some, perhaps imbued with shame, sought to move away, and so, having no further excuse to delay matters, the dejected Charles-Henri whipped up the horses and the carts continued on their way. And so another forty-five people were decapitated.

Meanwhile the leader and his colleagues had indeed been arrested and taken to gaol. However, within hours some of their sympathizers managed to effect their escape, Robespierre and his companions taking refuge in the Hôtel de Ville, the Commune headquarters. Soon the building was surrounded and fighting ensued between those trying to protect the fallen leader and those determined to recapture and execute him.

Eventually those with the latter intent gained the upper hand; entering the building they made their way to the second-floor room which held their enemies. In the furious mêlée that followed, Couthon was flung down the stairs, Augustin Robespierre threw himself from the window on to bayonets of the soldiers below and was badly injured, and

Henriot, former general of the National Guard, leapt from another window and hid in a sewer. One of the soldiers who discovered him stabbed him in the face, blinding him in one eye.

Lebas committed suicide by shooting himself, and Robespierre himself sustained a severely fractured jaw as the result of a pistol shot; whether this was caused by an attacker or a suicide bid was apparently never satisfactorily resolved, although later accounts reported that a gendarme named Charles-André Meda claimed to have fired the shot. Rewarded by promotion to colonel, and allegedly given a baronetcy, Meda later fought in the Napoleonic wars, dying of wounds received at Beresina.

All the prisoners were taken away, Robespierre being wheeled to the Tuileries on a hand barrow. There, after lying on a table for five hours subjected to the taunts and jeers of those who had once walked in terror of him, his wounds were dressed and he joined the others in the Conciergerie to await execution.

At their trial, the badly wounded Augustin was helped in between two gendarmes, two others carrying Couthon in an armchair. Robespierre himself said little, his injury preventing him from speaking coherently. After being sentenced to death, they were all taken to the Conciergerie.

Under Charles-Henri's supervision the prisoners were prepared, Sanson re-bandaging Robespierre's shattered jaw after cutting his hair, and at four o'clock that day, 28 July 1794, the twenty-one men descended the stairs to the courtyard, two dying men at the head of it, Lebas's corpse bringing up the rear.

In the cart Robespierre, his face swollen and livid, his hair awry, shirt torn and nankeen breeches stained with blood, sat on a pile of straw, apparently impervious to the vehement abuse of the crowds, while most of the others appeared shocked at the public's scorn. Only Dumas showed any venom; 'My only regret is that I did not get all these blackguards guillotined when I had the chance!' he exclaimed.

When the carts reached Robespierre's house they were brought to a standstill by the sheer mass of people blocking the road, people who formed rings around the cavalcade, dancing and singing. A child brought a bucket of blood from a neighbouring butcher's shop and the doors and walls of the house were daubed with it. Vainly Sanson tried to persuade the gendarmes to clear the way; he held no brief for Robespierre and the rest, but such inhumane displays sickened him. His efforts were in vain though, for the police joined the people in their celebrations, and it was some time before the road was cleared; and through it all, Robespierre sat unmoved, his eyes closed obviously in extreme pain.

It was 6.15 by the time the carts reached the Place de la Révolution and once there the convicts were led from the carts. One by one they were helped up the steps, Augustin having to be carried, as was Couthon, still in his armchair.

Robespierre was the tenth in line; climbing the steps unassisted, he exhibited neither bravado nor weakness. His close proximity to the guillotine seemed to hold no terrors for him; on the contrary, for in the past he had often stood and surveyed it, never imagining that he would ever be its victim. Deputy Dulaure once commented on it, saying:

> As for Robespierre, he seems not to have felt the least repulsion for this terrible instrument, which was an object of disgust and horror for nearly everyone. Far from shunning the sight of it, he frequently passed by that way in order to look at it; it almost seemed as though he took pleasure in it, for he stood still, it is said, when his walks led him to the end of the Champs-Elysées. This is far from being consistent with the sentiments of 'humanity' and 'sensibility' that he professed and was for ever talking about.

Now the fallen leader faced Sanson. His wound had been covered with a wet piece of linen, held in place by a thick napkin, another piece of linen surrounding his forehead and the back of his head, and the executioner, realizing that the material could well deflect the falling blade and cause unimaginable mutilation, ordered one of his assistants to remove it. This the man did, so brusquely that Robespierre uttered a fearful cry, the blood trickling down his chin, his mouth remaining wide open. His suffering lasted but a few seconds; instantly the weigh plank swung down, the blade was released – and the severed head was then shown to the people, in the same way as those of his previous victims, Danton, Desmoulins, and King Louis XVI.

The decapitated bodies were loaded on to the waiting tumbrils, the heads being placed separately in a chest; only Lebas's body escaped mutilation, and was conveyed in the third cart. Together all were transported to the cemetery of the Errancis where they were thrown into a trench dug in readiness. The cost of transport and burial amounted to 193 livres, with an additional sum of 7 livres given to the gravediggers, the total sum to include the supply of quicklime, a layer of which 'was spread over the remains of the tyrants, to prevent them from being deified in days to come'.

The bodies of other revolutionists were later buried there before the cemetery was finally closed, the word 'Sleep' being engraved above its never-opened door. As the years passed, most of the cemetery was cleared away, the site later being occupied by a tavern. This in turn disappeared beneath new roads which carved their way through the locality. What little undisturbed ground was left was enclosed by walls, where a few players of *boule* were wont to gather on Sunday afternoons, but by 1870 all had gone, fine houses having been erected upon that mournful spot.

A man who had a miraculous escape from death was Thomas Paine, a radical Englishman who had been elected deputy to represent the Pas-de-Calais in the Convention. He had voted with the Girondists and, by advocating that the King should be exiled to America rather than being executed, was imprisoned in 1794. Some months passed before he was put on the death-list and it so happened that when the turnkey came round to mark his cell door with chalk indicating his fate the next day, the door, which opened outwards, received the mark on its inner side. Later another turnkey came along and closed the door – and so the tumbril went without him! He was eventually released and, going to America, died in New York in 1809.

In the months that followed the death of Robespierre, minor officers of the regime were in turn brought to justice for the appalling crimes they had inflicted on the population. They were executed with few, if any, regrets by Charles-Henri and his assistants. Among them was

Representative Jean-Baptiste Carrier, a lawyer who was personally responsible for ordering the massacres which took place in the civil insurrection in the Vendée, thousands of French men, women and children being guillotined, shot or drowned. Deaths by the latter method were sadistically termed 'vertical deportations' or 'Republican Marriages', men and women being tied together hand and foot, then thrown into the river Loire.

The one-time president of the Tribunal, Hermann, met the death he had so cruelly meted out to others, and then, on 7 May 1795, Antoine Quentin Fouquier-Tinville himself, late Public Prosecutor of the Revolution, stepped on to Sanson's scaffold.

Like Couthon, he was a prime candidate for death, for with his cold and merciless devotion to what he saw as his duty, few had escaped his venomous condemnation. Here a labourer whistling an anti-republican tune, there a housewife criticizing the shortage of butter and eggs, all were denied leniency, all were grist to his murderous mill.

Contemporary writers described him as a heavily built man with a sallow complexion; his face was pitted with smallpox, his hair was dark, his forehead narrow, his eyes small and glittering. In court he wore a black coat with a small cape, a white cravat and a broad-brimmed hat adorned with a tricolour cockade and large black plumes, a medal engraved with the fasces and the Phrygian cap of liberty being his only decoration.

His only relaxation was to see his victims suffer on the scaffold; then his grim features would melt for a moment and even soften into a smile, expressive of the delight he experienced in the spectacle. He coveted no luxuries, and as money held no lure, attempts to bribe him were wasted. As his only enjoyment was that of causing people to be put to death and then watching them die, he knew that mere wealth could never replace that gratification. Judging by his record, and the opinion held by Charles-Henri, his contemporaries were probably right.

When, to the deafening applause of the crowd jostling for advantageous positions around the scaffold, he faced the executioner, the man he had so often reprimanded and threatened, he snarled, 'Villain! I thought I would be sending you to the place you are taking me!' adding, 'I see no reason why they shouldn't condemn the executioner; one is as guilty as the other!'

As Charles-Henri gave the signal for the release of the blade, no doubt that thought crossed his mind also, probably not for the first time. Miraculously, unaccountably, he had survived the Revolution; yet its scars would sear his mind and conscience until his dying day.

7 Faces in Wax

Such is the macabre curiosity inherent in human nature that in most countries public executions invariably attracted large crowds. Morbid-minded spectators, ghoulish thrill-seekers or just inquisitive passers-by flocked around the scaffold, there to watch the victim struggle in his death-throes at the end of a rope, scream as his limbs were shattered on the wheel or watch the blood gush forth as the sword or guillotine blade severed the head from the body.

But what of those who, perhaps having arrived late on the scene or due to the sheer size of the crowd, did not manage to get a clear view of the ghastly proceedings – or for whatever reason, were unable to attend at all? Admittedly reports of the execution would possibly be published in the news-sheets on the following day, but the most graphic and detailed description would hardly compensate for the total absence of pictures in those pre-photographic days.

This deficiency was overcome, as far as Paris society was concerned, by a doctor named Philip Curtius. He was born at Nockach, on the Rhine, on 30 January 1737, reportedly the child of Christopher Frederick Curtius and his wife Catherine Mauret. Contemporary writers however averred that he was a German named Kurtz who later adopted the name Curtius. Be that as it may, at the age of twenty-three he not only had a medical practice in Berne, Switzerland, but had developed a creative ability for sculpting in wax, talents which he combined by skilfully modelling human organs in that substance and selling them to anatomists and medical schools for use in training would-be surgeons.

Possessing a flair for innovation and an eye for a profit-making venture, he extended his capabilities into the field of portraiture, exploiting the conceit of the wealthy by modelling live masks of them, creating three-dimensional images of greater similitude than any oil painting. These masks were made by spreading fine plaster of Paris over the sitter's face, straws in the nostrils permitting breathing to continue. When the mask had set and been removed, clay was squeezed into it, taking on the delineations of the sitter's features. This would be built up into a head, forming the basis for a two-piece mould which was then filled with melted wax. When the wax had formed an outer crust about one and a half inches thick, the surplus was poured away and the mould removed. The wax head would then be painted with life-like detail and, after hair and eyes had been added, would present an almost perfect replica of the sitter.

It was at one of his exhibitions that the Bourbon prince, Louis de Conti, cousin of the French King, noticed and admired the excellence of Curtius's work, and suggested that Paris might be a more profitable location for future exhibitions. The Prince went further, offering to install Curtius in suitable studios in that city.

The backing of such an influential figure was not to be rejected out of hand, and so shortly afterwards Curtius moved to Paris, at first living in the Hôtel d'Allegre on the rue St Honoré. The sculptures he created for his new patron led to such an enthusiastic response from the rich members of French society that Curtius decided to set up his headquarters and workshop permanently in that city, and in 1767 he established a gallery in the fashionable *quartier* nearby, a showroom in which he displayed the busts of famous personalities of the day.

Curtius had a sister, Marie Grosholtz, who had married a Swiss officer, Joseph Grosholtz, aide-de-camp to General Wurmser during the Seven Years' War. During a campaign he had been severely wounded, his skull being injured and his lower jaw shot away, and in 1761 he died, leaving his widow pregnant. The baby, born two months later in Strasburg, was also christened Marie, and mother and daughter later moved to Berne.

They were frequently visited by Philip Curtius who, being unmarried, eventually invited the two Maries to join him in Paris. This they did in 1766, the 5-year-old proving to be a bright and intelligent girl who enjoyed helping her Uncle

Philip in the gallery and, child-like, also played with the clay liberally available in the workshop. Such was the natural propensity she showed for shaping and manipulating the medium, that Curtius gave her tuition, training to which she soon responded by displaying a remarkable ability in the craft.

Meanwhile the doctor had further expanded his display to include not only busts, but complete figures, accurately clothed and arranged in appropriate settings; royalty in the throne-room, politicians haranguing their colleagues. His gallery was visited by the artistic coterie of the city, painters and poets, writers and dilettantes, who would sit and discuss the vital issues of the day.

Marie, now in her twenties, had grown up to be a slim, attractive girl, her large eyes, sharp nose and somewhat pointed chin indicative of her lively and intelligent nature. She was proving so excellent a sculptor that her work attracted the attention of none other than King Louis XVI's sister, the Princess Elizabeth, who, eager to learn wax modelling at first hand, invited Marie to reside in the palace of Versailles to teach her royal patron. This Marie did, though still visiting her mother and uncle frequently.

As his business thrived, Curtius, an entrepreneur by nature, opened another gallery in 1770, this time in the Boulevard du Temple and, desirous of some new type of display which would tempt more customers, became aware of the popularity of public floggings, the pillory and in particular, executions. And so he developed the idea, modelling with great accuracy and attention to detail, the faces and figures of notorious criminals, not only in the act of performing their dastardly deeds but also while receiving their just deserts.

These tableaux, displayed in what he called his *Caverne des Voleurs*, Cave of Thieves, were an instant success with the public, but such was Curtius's insistence on reproducing the exact features of the criminals he modelled, every wart and wrinkle, that difficulties arose in finding out precisely what they looked like. The solution was obvious; befriend the city's executioner and, crudely, do a deal.

At that time, as mentioned earlier, Charles-Henri was experiencing, in modern terminology, cash-flow problems.

His salary was not being paid promptly, his debtors were badgering him, his expenses were increasing. The approach by Dr Curtius also offered another opportunity; always ambitious to be recognized as a man of substance, an officer of Parliament, rather than the despised common hangman, acceptance into the fashionable circles of Curtius's gallery would bring him the respectability he felt was his due. And so the agreement was made. He, Charles-Henri, would advise and assist, would allow the doctor and his talented niece Marie to take death masks of noted villains as soon as possible after their execution, either in the temporary morgue adjoining his house, or *en route* to the cemeteries.

When civil unrest threatened in 1789, Curtius, although a royalist by instinct, saw which way the wind was blowing and decided that a change of allegiance would not only safeguard his profitable business but, if the worst came to the worst, his neck; and as a necessary expedient he insisted that Marie end her nine-year association with the royal family forthwith and return to assist him in the gallery and the workshop.

Moreover, to demonstrate his adherence to the reactionary opinions rife in the city, his guests would no longer be the artistic élite, but those who preached the revolutionary solution to the nation's ills. Marie therefore occasionally found herself acting as hostess to Robespierre, Desmoulins, Marat and the like as they gathered in hot discussion around the table. In her *Mémoires* published in 1838 she described how she had found Robespierre extremely polite and attentive, never omitting those little acts of courtesy expected of a gentleman; animated in conversation, she said, but his enunciation not well formed. With great perception, she also commented that although he boasted of living meagrely on fifteen pence a day, he was 'a very libidinous man, and circumstances must have occurred, in the course of his transactions with his fair favourites, which demanded money which there is no doubt he must have found means of raising and supplying'! Little could she imagine that there would come a day when she would hold the decapitated heads of her uncle's guests in order to obtain their death masks.

The partnership with Sanson proceeded satisfactorily. There being nearly 130 offences punishable under the law on the statute books at that time, business was brisk, and such was the celerity with which Marie Grosholtz could fashion the amazing likenesses of the latest robber or murderer in the process of being tortured or executed, together with Curtius's skill in depicting the appropriate setting, that most mornings would find queues lining up along the Boulevard du Temple, eager to see the punishment which had been inflicted only hours earlier, portrayed in wax.

When it became obvious to Curtius that the political situation was deteriorating, he joined the National Guard, a citizen army raised to counter the Royal Guard, and as an officer he led his troops in the attack on the Bastille on 14 July 1789. As mentioned earlier, the Governor, the Marquis de Launay, was beheaded by the mob, and Marie modelled his death mask, which was later displayed in the *Caverne des Voleurs*.

With the Revolution well under way, Curtius became an active member, the brunt of the gallery work falling on Marie's shoulders, and with the introduction of the guillotine in 1792 she found herself taking death masks each night of those executed, not only revolutionaries such as Charlotte Corday, Hébert and Marat, Carrier and the repulsive Fouquier-Tinville, but also of Louis XVI and Marie Antoinette. The latter task must have been particularly disturbing for her, for she had known and liked the members of the royal family while living in the palace of Versailles. The storming of the Tuileries also had a traumatic effect on her emotions, for among the hundreds of Swiss Guard massacred by the mob were her three brothers and two of her uncles. All were cut to pieces.

As the political temperature rose, and anyone who murmured against the Revolution lost their head, it was inevitable that accusing fingers should be pointed at Marie Grosholtz because of her association with the Princess Elizabeth. One day, to her horror, she was arrested at the gallery and taken to the prison of La Force. The food was inadequate and stale, the bedding consisted of straw spread on the floor, and every few days she and her fellow prisoners had their hair clipped short in readiness for execution. For the three months of her imprisonment she lived in fearful trepidation that, any day, like so many others whose features she had modelled, she too would have to join her friend Charles-Henri on the scaffold, to have HER head removed. But either through Dr Curtius's influence with his army superiors, or the sudden denunciation and execution of Robespierre, she was released, and therefore was able to continue her gruesome work, including that of modelling the great leader's head in the cemetery.

On 13 August 1794 Curtius died, aged fifty-seven, and Marie became the sole owner of the famous *Caverne* with its 'living' tableaux. Some time later, in September 1795, she fell in love with a man seven years younger than herself. Born in Mâcon in Burgundy, he was a member of a long-established family of metalworkers and though at one time he had been a wine-grower, when Marie met him he was an engineer. Marie married François, and so changed her name to one which was to become recognized world-wide – Madame Marie Tussaud.

But by now the Revolution had ended and, the public having had a plethora of blood and mutilation, attendance at the gallery waned. Nor was this the only misfortune, for although the Tussauds raised a family of three children, the marriage was not a success. In 1802 Marie left her husband in Paris and, packing her irreplaceable moulds and models, she left for England.

There she created a museum which has subsequently provided much entertainment to the countless thousands of people who, 200 years later, queue, not on the Boulevard du Temple to marvel at the *Caverne des Voleurs*, but on Marylebone Road, London, there to shudder on seeing the Chamber of Horrors in Madame Tussaud's waxworks museum. And whatever repugnance or revulsion may be felt about the French Revolution in general or the executioner in particular, it should be remembered that this world-famous collection could not have existed, had it not been for the assistance given by Monsieur de Paris, Charles-Henri Sanson!

8   Charles-Henri: The Declining Years

The execution of Robespierre and his supporters signalled the end of the Revolution, but France, weary with the bloodshed, low in spirit and short of essential foods, still looked in vain for firm government. In October 1795 an insurrection occurred in Paris, this being quelled by an artillery officer named Bonaparte who, stamping his considerable authority on the political situation, would later rule the country as Emperor Napoleon.

For his part, Charles-Henri had run his course. Weary, mentally exhausted, the strain of executing nearly three thousand people over the last few years had finally started to take its toll, and he developed nephritis, a kidney complaint. On 30 October 1795 he retired, leaving his son Henri in charge of the scaffold, though the younger man would not receive his formal commission until his father's death.

Charles-Henri submitted a claim for an annual pension of one thousand francs, stating that he had been in office since 1754, when his father Jean-Baptiste had retired, and so had served for forty-one years as executioner. His retirement was agreed to, his claim for a pension was not. Some years later an interdepartmental letter between the Treasury and the Minister of Justice stated:

> Citizen Sanson, formerly Executioner of Criminal Sentences, after obtaining leave to retire in 1795, now claims a pension for his services. It appears from the documents forwarded with his claim that he was not *officially* appointed executioner until 1 February 1778. He has therefore served less than the thirty years required by law which would entitle him to a pension. It is true that he professes to be suffering from some complaint.

Charles-Henri and Marie-Anne moved out of Paris to their house in Brie-Comte-Robert. His grandson, Henri-Clement, was later to recall his memories of the old man walking each morning in the well-tended garden, indulging himself in the only occupation which gave him pleasure.

I can still see him with his three-cornered hat, his knee breeches and thin bladed sword [Henri-Clement wrote]. He used to stop before the flowers he had cultivated himself, and he looked at them with something like tenderness. One day I remember that he exclaimed before a number of tulips of finest red, 'How fresh, how red they are! If they saw them they would say that I water them with blood!' Young as I was, the words struck me. Some days before I had heard an absurd vampire story which had left a deep impression on my mind. Somehow the two ideas got together in my head and I could not help asking my mother, 'Mamma, grandfather says he waters the flowers with blood; is it because he is a vampire?' My mother started; 'Be quiet, be quiet!' she exclaimed. 'Who told you those nasty things?' She made me promise not to say any more about it, and the circumstances passed from my mind, but later I understood what my grandfather had meant.

Henri Sanson, Charles-Henri's son, assumed the duties of Monsieur de Paris, albeit unofficially, and doubtless welcomed the decrease in the numbers to be guillotined. By now the victims were those who, it could be said, really deserved it, the murderers, rapists and other criminals. Even they were few, and those committing lesser crimes meant that the pillory and branding iron were employed more than the guillotine.

One case, in 1796, which, despite the past horrors, did capture the public's attention, also brought Charles-Henri out of retirement to assist his son. It was known as 'The Affair of the Lyons Mail' and it involved a gang of robbers who for many months had been terrorizing a large area of countryside near Orléans, resisting all efforts to capture them. They were known as *Les Chauffeurs*, the Warmers, because in order to discover the whereabouts of people's valuables, they would light a fire and proceed to roast their

victim's feet at it until the required information was forthcoming.

A far more serious crime however was laid at their door when the Lyons mail coach was ambushed by highwaymen. The courier and postillion were brutally murdered and the contents of the coach stolen. Pressure was brought to bear on the authorities and shortly afterwards a man called Courriol was arrested, letters and cash from the mail having been found in his possession. Two other men, Golier and Guesno, were also thought to be implicated but, no evidence being offered against the latter, he was released.

While he was on his way to the Prefecture to collect his passport which had been impounded, he met a friend, one Lesurques, and while still continuing to recount what had happened, Guesno led the way into the police office, accompanied by his friend.

It was then that an appalling coincidence occurred, for at the time two women, who had witnessed the attack on the mail coach, were being questioned by the police and as Guesno and Lesurques walked in, the women immediately identified them as two of the murderers!

In vain both men protested their innocence. Both were arrested and put on trial. Lesurques produced fifteen witnesses to vouch for his whereabouts at the time in question, but even these alibis were discredited when one of his witnesses, a jeweller named Le Grand, was called to confirm that he had transacted business with Lesurques on the day of the crime. Upon producing his record book it was noticed that an eight had been altered to a nine, thus casting doubt on the rest of the alibi. Relevant or not, from that moment Lesurques was a doomed man.

When the jury retired to consider its verdict, a woman named Madeleine Brebant stood up in the body of the court and, declaring herself to be the mistress of Courriol, swore that Lesurques and Guesno were indeed innocent; that the two women in the Prefecture had been deceived by the fatal resemblance both men bore to the real murderers, whom she named as Vidal and Dubosc.

The judge however proved adamant in his refusal to countenance any further evidence, and the jury returned, having found Curriol and Lesurques guilty, and Guesno innocent. The plea to free Lesurques was now taken up by Curriol who, to his credit, swore that the attack was carried out by himself and the two men named by his mistress. He went so far in his efforts to exonerate the unfortunate man that he even wrote to the *Directoire* in Paris. They set up a committee to look into the matter but, no real effort being made to investigate, the plea was rejected.

On 30 October 1796 Charles-Henri and his son Henri went as usual to the Conciergerie to collect their prisoners. Courriol was still frantically trying to save Lesurques who by now appeared resigned to his fate. He handed Charles-Henri a note, saying, 'Be good enough to keep this letter, which may hereafter contribute to the honour of my wife and my poor children so unjustly deprived of husband and father.'

As young Henri was cutting Lesurques's hair, Charles-Henri read the letter, which was directed to the man actually responsible for the murders:

> To Citizen Dubosc; I do not even know you, and I am going to suffer the death which was reserved for you. Be satisfied with the sacrifice of my life. Should you ever be brought to account, remember my three children and their mother, who are disgraced for ever. Do not prolong their agony, but confess that you are the man.
>
> Signed, Lesurques

Charles-Henri promised he would circulate the contents of the letter to the newspapers, and then led the two men to the waiting cart. Every few yards along the route Curriol continued his exhortations by shouting, 'I alone am guilty – Lesurques is innocent!' On the scaffold, his voice going higher and higher, he repeated his cry, and Charles-Henri stated that the very thud of the blade drowned the sound of Curriol's final plea for justice to be done.

Lesurques, dressed in spotless white, as a symbol of his innocence, silently allowed himself to be strapped to the weigh plank. Then, just before the blade was released, he exclaimed, 'May God forgive my judges as I forgive them!' And Charles-Henri, long attuned to the tones of sincerity or otherwise of his victims, turned to his son and said, 'The man is innocent; we have executed an innocent man.'

Four years later Vidal and Dubosc were captured. The latter criminal denied any complicity in the murders, but another member of the gang, named Roussy, made a full confession and exonerated Lesurques completely.

It was too late for Lesurques, and even too late for his mother and his wife. Their property had been confiscated and both women became mentally deranged. His mother died in an asylum, though his wife recovered some years later. It was not until twenty-five years had passed that the authorities bowed to public opinion and the efforts made by representatives of the family, when the Ministry of Finances at last accepted that the confiscation of Lesurques's property was illegal, and it was duly restored to the children.

On only one other occasion did Charles-Henri visit the scaffold. On 19 March 1803 a grocer named Trumeau was found guilty of poisoning his daughter and his niece with arsenic. As at the execution of Lesurques, the old man's innate sense of discernment convinced him of Trumeau's innocence, but no last-minute reprieve was forthcoming and Trumeau suffered beneath the blade. It was not until many years later that fresh evidence emerged to exonerate the grocer, and young Henri, on poring over his father's register one day, came across the comment written alongside Trumeau's entry, 'Again a Lesurques.'

During the following year, Charles-Henri, now sixty-six, and Marie-Anne, moved back into their house at No. 10 rue Neuve Saint Jean in Paris. During the following months his health started to deteriorate, and he was eventually confined to his bed. His son Henri frequently visited him, accompanied by his wife, Marie-Louise, and their child, Henri-Clement, and although in pain, Charles-Henri's spirit was still strong enough to refute his son's contention that Henri-Clement, when old enough, should seek another occupation. 'Do nothing of the kind!' he exclaimed forcefully. 'If he takes up a different career he'll despise all of us!'

On 4 July 1806 Marie-Anne realized that the end was near and sent for Henri. Just before his death Charles-Henri called his son to his side and said:

Henri, I am going away, and I have to say a few parting

words before I die. I am aware that you never liked your profession; I think however that I leave you a good example. Believe me, let us abide by the station which fate awarded to us. It is of no use to hope that the world will ever receive you; your origin can neither be forgotten nor forgiven.

Do not take another occupation for yourself or your son. It would be a desertion from your duty. There has not been a single instance in our family of such a desertion. Our family is certainly the most ancient and important in the profession; but others have done as we have done.

For a long time I sincerely believed that we were very useful to society, and that in no profession were self-denial and devotion shown more than in ours, but I have seen such singular events that my opinions are slightly altered now. Some day we may be suppressed, just as many other things have been suppressed. Until then be certain that no one has a right to blame or insult you. You are not responsible for the blood you shed. Do not forget that the judge who passes sentence is more responsible than you are.

The funeral service, attended by relatives, friends and officials of the courts and council, took place in the church of Saint Laurent, and because the decree forbidding burials within the confines of churches was being stringently observed, the burial took place at Montmartre.

In his memoirs his grandson, Henri-Clement, recalled how, although only seven years old at the time

as the funeral procession passed by, the people were quiet and almost sympathetic, but when we went up the hill towards Montmartre there were mutterings, and I heard someone ask whose funeral it was, and the man replied, with a strange sort of look, that it was the hangman's. I felt my father's hand tighten on mine, and I realized that that was the first time I had heard THAT word. Although I didn't know what it actually meant, some mysterious instinct made me feel that it would be the bane of my life.

Charles-Henri was interred in the cemetery at Montmartre, a headstone later being erected, engraved with the words which, loosely translated, read; 'This stone was erected by his son and family, by whom his passing was regretted.'

9   Henri

Henri was born on Christmas Eve 1767 and, just as his
forebears had done, was soon inducted into the ways of the
scaffold, being present during executions from the young
age of eleven. Despite the revulsion he felt at having to be
an executioner, with the consequential rejection by society,
he had always been proud of his father's integrity, and in
particular the fierce way in which Charles-Henri had
defended the honourable position of the executioner in the
nation's life. He recalled how, when the Abbé Maury had
viciously attacked the profession in a session of the National
Assembly by saying, 'Every honest man shudders at the
sight of one who murders his fellow-creatures in cold blood,
but does the law order a man to be an executioner?', adding
that those of such a discreditable calling should be deprived
of the civil rights enjoyed by everyone else, his father had
immediately refuted the accusation by letter to the
Assembly:

> Gentlemen; For a long time the executioners of criminal
> judgements have complained of the injustice of a prejudice
> which partly awards to them the disgrace of the crimes which
> justice punishes through their instrumentality. They have
> hitherto suffered the humiliation, but have found sufficient
> consolation in their consciences. It is now attempted to
> sanction this prejudice by declaring them unfit to hold civil
> rights. Such is, at least, the intention expressed by the Abbé
> Maury at the last sitting of the Assembly.
>   The Abbé Maury's motion has caused us considerable
> alarm, and we are convinced that justice must be deprived of
> its executive strength if the motion is carried.
>   The executioner of Paris, Charles-Henri Sanson, who

hereby presents to you his most respectful remonstrances, declares – and all his confrères will follow his example – that he will tender his resignation if you declare that executioners are not citizens.

The petitioner trusts that you will deign to examine the question with the attention it deserves. At a time when justice prevails, you will not suffer it to be overlooked.

Signed, SANSON, etc.

That his father should stand up to the might of the Assembly on behalf of all the executioners did him nothing but credit, for his point of view was accepted by the Assembly; nevertheless Henri knew that he could never accept the job whole-heartedly, especially after the awful occasion on which he had had to carry the body of his younger brother, Gabriel, after the youth's fatal fall from the scaffold.

However, he realized that he could not withstand his fate, though his somewhat fatalistic nature, coupled with an ability to mentally disassociate himself to some extent from what he was doing, would doubtless sustain him. Which it did, although because of that he was sometimes accused of indifference to his victims' sufferings during the 360 or more executions over which he officiated.

His really active role had commenced with the introduction of the guillotine in 1792, and he was present when Charles-Henri carried out the trials on the sheep and corpses in the Bicetre hospital. From then on he had assisted his father almost continually, as a member of the team administering the victims' toilette prior to their boarding the tumbrils, and subsequently on the scaffold. He it was who supported Madame du Barry during her last journey, and also upon whose foot Marie Antoinette accidentally stepped; at his exclamation, she reportedly said, 'Pardon, Monsieur!' Moments later, as recounted earlier, it was Henri who secured her to the bascule and released the blade.

At some time during the Revolution Henri married. Perhaps because of the existing chaotic conditions, or because only a civil ceremony may have been conducted, no record of the wedding between himself and Marie-Louise

Damidot exists. She was a bright and attractive girl from a respectable family and, having been born on 14 October 1776, was nearly ten years younger than her new husband. Little is known of her reasons for marrying into a dynasty of such unfavourable repute, but she was evidently devoted to Henri, and bore him four children. The eldest, Henri-Clement, destined to be the last in the Sanson dynasty of executioners of Paris, was born in 1799. He had two sisters, Marie-Gabrielle, born in 1802, and Adelaide, born in 1804. True to the family tradition, both chose executioners as their partners, Marie-Gabrielle marrying Monsieur de Lyons, Adelaide marrying Monsieur de Versailles. And in 1810 Nicolas Eugene was born, but of his life nothing is known.

One Sunday in October 1793 Henri attended church as usual and afterwards, while conversing with friends, was flattered when he was invited, not only to join a company of gunners which was being formed, but to become one of their officers. At the meeting which followed, he was elected captain of the 48th Company of the Paris Artillery Corps, and one of his uncles, Pierre-Charles, who was present, was made a sub-lieutenant. Although totally lacking in military knowledge, Henri was not too proud to admit his ignorance to the sergeant of the company, who instructed him in the basic principles of warfare.

His ability to command the fifty-one men of his company was soon put to the test when an insurrection in La Brie against the Revolution had to be put down, but this was achieved without being involved in any actual fighting. From his own account he enjoyed military life, with its strict disciplines; by now he was a tall and well-built man and in his uniform of a blue tunic with yellow facings, and black bicorn hat adorned with a red pompon, must have cut a dashing figure indeed.

Shortly afterwards he was temporarily transferred to the gendarmerie, and in that role found himself escorting, rather than riding in, the tumbrils. At other times he was among those who lined the route and, on 21 January 1793, was on duty near the scaffold when his father and uncles guillotined the King.

Some time later he reverted to the artillery, and it was then that the unthinkable all but happened; the terrifying possibility that he, a Sanson, might actually end up on the scaffold, not as the executioner, but strapped to the bascule and beheaded!

On the advent of the power struggle between Robespierre's faction and the rest of the Convention, Henri and his uncle, the lieutenant, were ordered by the adjutant general to proceed with their two cannon, twenty-five gunners and thirty foot soldiers and take up positions in the Place de Grève, one of the main squares of the city. No one knew the reason for such a display of arms, and wild rumours were circulated that either Robespierre had gained the ascendancy or had been arrested.

The two officers were then told to report to the police headquarters; on doing so, they were required to sign the attendance register, as was the normal practice. Shortly afterwards the news came that Robespierre had been overthrown. Henri's position was now exceedingly delicate. The fallen leader had been extremely popular with the police, and his downfall put all those even remotely connected with the force in extreme danger. As Henri himself said, 'When there is discord between different authorities who constitute public power, the officer, whose mission it is to obey, is much perplexed. At such a time of anarchy, officers are exposed to becoming the blind instruments of one faction or the other, and that is just what happened to me.'

Alarmed by the turn of events, he and his uncle hastily returned to their unit, but they had been observed in the company of those who supported Robespierre. Thus compromised, Henri, his uncle, and forty-one alleged accomplices were arrested and charged with offering active support to the renegade faction. Denials were brushed aside; their presence in the headquarters, as evidenced by their signatures on the register sheet, was damning.

They were taken to the Conciergerie prison, where Henri was locked up in the very cell in which Marie Antoinette had been incarcerated and indeed, slept in the bed which she had occupied, a unique privilege which no doubt he would gladly have forgone. At his trial he was defended effectively, being able to prove that neither he nor his company had had any intention of interceding and in fact had not stirred from their allotted location. The Tribunal, its fearsome attitude now mellowed somewhat by the fall of Robespierre, accepted that no witnesses could be produced to corroborate complicity with those opposing the Convention. Henri and his uncle were acquitted.

The fortunate young man later related how

> When we were discharged, I ran to a room in the Palais de Justice where I knew my father was waiting anxiously for the outcome of the trial. I embraced him, weeping with joy, but I was surprised to find a cloud over his countenance. Alas, I had forgotten that out of the forty-one prisoners, forty had been acquitted, but the forty-first, Joseph Lemonnier, Civil Commissioner and captain in the National Guard, was to die the following day.

Despite this narrow escape, Henri felt the call of a military career almost overwhelming. To hold his head up high in society, to be respected as an officer instead of being scorned and despised as a hangman, was a prize much sought after. But, as was the way in such a close-knit family as theirs, he listened to his father's words:

> It is your turn to take on the responsibility and trust that belongs to our family. The position will bring you more than twelve thousand livres a year; you will be wise to take it, my boy. You must understand that the prejudice against us will always exist and will prevent you from advancing in rank; it may even deprive you of the rank of captain. This way, our way, you will live in peace, with no one having the right to meddle in your affairs.

Rather than risk stagnating without prospect of promotion or, worse, being cashiered, Henri made up his mind and resigned his commission. On 30 October 1795, Charles-Henri having retired, he assumed control of the scaffold, the public prosecutor attached to the criminal tribunal of the Seine issuing the necessary authority:

> The post of Executioner of Criminal Sentences in Paris being rendered vacant by the resignation of Charles-Henri Sanson, the Commune, in accordance with the law of 13 June 1793,

has given the commission to Henri Sanson, son of the late holder of the office, whose name is on the list of candidates capable of carrying out the duties....

Henri would not, however, be formally appointed until his father's death in 1806.

Now that the Revolution had ended, his duties were more mundane, by far the majority of his victims being common criminals. And so Henri, 'a big red-faced bald-headed man in a black frock coat and three cornered hat' as described by Victor Hugo, supervised his assistants as they administered the punishments decreed by the courts. Whipping was still the penalty for counterfeiting and other offences; the branding iron was also much in demand, albeit not by the recipients. The letters and numbers burned into the shoulders of offenders varied, depending on their crime. Mention has already been made of the letter 'V', *voleuse*, with which Comtesse de la Motte was branded; among the others were 'T' for a time sentence and 'TP' for a life sentence.

Forgers were identified by 'F' being seared on the shoulders of those sentenced to imprisonment or hard labour, 'TF' (*travaux forcés*) for those sentenced to penal servitude, 'TPF' (*travaux à perpétuité*) being reserved for forgers starting penal servitude for life.

These letters, one inch in height, were preceded by numbers of the same size, indicating the *départment* in which the particular prison was situated. Immediately after the branding iron had burned the flesh, an ointment consisting of lard and crushed gunpowder was applied to the victim's shoulder with a piece of wood padded with leather. It was thought that this ointment would replace tattooing and so would make the brand indelible, but this proved not to be the case, for the burn would not heal without scabbing, and once the scab came away, the new skin was as white as that surrounding it. These brands were in use until 21 June 1811, the numbers being abolished on 25 March 1820.

When his Paris duties permitted, Henri occasionally went further afield, on one occasion in 1797 helping his uncle Nicolas Charles Gabriel, executioner of Blois, to guillotine François Noel Babeuf, a communist who, with others of a similar persuasion, not only planned to establish a communist system in the country, but also plotted to destroy the government.

Among the many other conspiracies in those republican days was one engineered by Georges Cadoudal and General Charles Pichegru. Cadoudal, a miller's son from Lower Brittany, was a fervent supporter of the royal house of the Bourbons; Pichegru achieved military distinction and fame until he swore fealty to the royalist cause. In 1797 the latter was arrested and banished to Cayenne, but escaped and made his way to London. In 1804 he linked up with Cadoudal in Paris, there to plan Napoleon's assassination, but both were betrayed and captured; Pichegru was confined in the Temple prison, where he was found strangled in bed. Cadoudal and eleven accomplices had the doubtful pleasure of meeting Henri Sanson on the scaffold, there to be guillotined.

But perhaps the most sensational case of the time was that involving Manette Bonhourt, an attractive and exuberant blonde who was dubbed *La fille Bonhourt* by the Paris press, though she did in fact call herself by the masculine name of 'Auguste', because of her habit of wearing men's clothing. Not any male attire, but a most striking ensemble, consisting of a shiny top hat and a figure-hugging coat, below which she wore tight white breeches and long leather boots, an outrageous and eye-catching outfit in that particular, or indeed any, day and age.

Some years earlier she had had a love affair, one which she had only allowed to become intimate on the understanding that the man concerned would marry her. When alas he jilted her, she promptly swore revenge on all men, and carefully laid her plans. Clad in her spectacular costume, she would lure a man to an hotel room, and there order drinks. Seizing the moment, Manette would then pour a soporific powder into his glass and as soon as the man lost consciousness, take a hammer from the beaded bag she carried and strike her prey a single, fatal blow on the left temple.

Having removed all the money, rings and other valuables from the body, she then spent the night there. In the morning she would leave, allaying any suspicion by announcing to the desk clerk on the way out that she was going shopping, and that her 'husband' was not to be disturbed until she returned at lunch-time. So bemused were hotel staff by this dazzling creature that on the discovery of the corpse and the continued absence of his shapely companion, no reliable description was ever forthcoming. Manette meanwhile changed into more feminine garb and melted into the Parisian boulevards.

As the years passed and the number of her victims exceeded five, then ten, even fifteen, the police eventually resorted to desperate measures by detailing one of their men to act as decoy. After some weeks he managed to meet Manette in a bar, and accompanied her to an hotel. Despite being on the alert, he was duped into drinking the drugged contents of the glass she handed him; even as he felt his senses reeling he managed to call for assistance and, when the hotel staff rushed in, succeeded in arresting her, doubtless before falling asleep!

In court she evinced not the slightest sense of guilt or remorse, boasting instead that she had killed about twenty men in revenge, and even a girl whom she thought had suspected her real identity. She was found guilty and sentenced to death, but the idea that such a gorgeous female should be guillotined, for whatever crime, was anathema to the French. Petitions urging clemency were raised, and applications for a reduction of sentence were submitted to the Emperor's office. Some high-level considerations must evidently have taken place for, contrary to the usual practice, the appeal court took two years to deliver its findings, only to confirm that Manette Bonhourt should die.

When, on 16 May 1808, Henri Sanson and his assistants went to the Conciergerie to collect their prisoner, they found her dressed once more in her outrageous uniform, her costume of vengeance. Her long blonde tresses were quickly shorn and her wrists tied behind her. On the scaffold, before the crowds who had waited long hours to see such a celebrity executed, Manette was led to the guillotine by Henri. As they stopped in front of the weigh plank she turned to him. 'Don't you think it a pity,' she murmured coquettishly, 'to have to cut off a head as beautiful as mine?' Then just before the bascule swung downwards, she noticed the lustful expressions on the faces of the men clustered around the scaffold. 'Look at the vicious lot,' she exclaimed furiously. 'They'd rather have seen me stripped for a whipping!'

Far worse than straightforward execution was that inflicted on three men, Carbonneau, Pleignier and Tolleron who, following the restoration of the monarchy, plotted to assassinate King Louis XVIII. The penal code at that time stipulated that 'a man condemned to death for regicide shall be led to the place of execution in his shirt sleeves, barefoot, his head covered with a black veil. He shall stand on the scaffold while the bailiff shall read out his sentence; he shall then have his right hand amputated and immediately thereafter be executed'.

Sanson, being no butcher, left his assistants to perform this abhorrent task: young Henri-Clement could not even bring himself to be a spectator, remaining instead at the foot of the scaffold steps.

In between his scaffold appearances Henri was very much the archetypal family man. Regular meals, and games with the children, were very much the order of the day, the novelist Honoré de Balzac describing him as 'severe and reticent, with a highly developed sense of propriety'. His dress reflected his sober mien, for he wore a black suit, his only concession to fashion being a pleated white jabot, his air of respectability heightened by the solid gold watch-chain he wore across his middle.

Nor did the household consist solely of his wife and children. Kind and hospitable towards his relatives, Henri extended the shelter of his home not only to his elderly mother Marie-Anne, after Charles-Henri died, but also to Marie-Victoire, the widow of his uncle, Louis Charles Martin, and Mademoiselle Lexcellent, her daughter by a previous marriage.

As with most families of that era, the Sanson boys tended to adopt the hobbies and pursuits of their fathers, and Henri's musical tastes included playing the piano, at which he became quite proficient. Having received a good education, he became fluent in the English language, enjoying reading the more serious literature of the day.

It need hardly be said that, like his ancestors, Henri practised medicine, dispensing ointments and potions to his many clients, though it is doubtful whether his cure for rheumatism included as an ingredient, fat taken from a hanged man!

An event which saddened all the members of the family occurred on 24 October 1817 when Marie-Anne passed away peacefully in her sleep at the age of eighty-four. Such was the understanding and devotion with which she sustained her husband during the horrifying years of the Terror, that she must surely, in her own way, have been entitled to share her husband's title of 'Le Grand'.

The death, expected as it may have been, brought grief to the Sansons and their relatives, the immediate family going into deep mourning. All planned entertainments were immediately cancelled, curtains at the windows being drawn, and black clothing worn as a sign of their bereavement.

Henri's health was generally good, but in 1819 he suffered an attack of pleurisy which laid him low for a couple of months. During this time his place was taken by his son Henri-Clement, now aged twenty, whose reactions to the onerous task are described in the next chapter.

Once back on his feet, Henri's life continued as before, supervising the punishment and execution of those sentenced by the courts.

Few of his executions were noteworthy until, in 1822, yet another conspiracy to overthrow the Bourbon royal family was uncovered, this time within the ranks of the army. A secret society had infiltrated the service and had influenced those dissatisfied with their royal rulers. One such splinter group was discovered in the 45th Regiment, led by a sergeant named Bories, a tall and eloquent man whose dedication to the rebel cause fired the imagination of his fellow soldiers, who willingly accepted the symbol of the society, the dagger.

Their naïve enthusiasm was so openly expressed that the suspicions of their superiors were quickly aroused. Goupillon, one of the youngest plotters, revealed their secret plans to the colonel of the regiment, resulting in the arrest of the twenty-five men involved. Of the soldiers, those most senior in rank were Bories and Pommier, sergeant-majors, and Goubin, Raoulx and Amis, sergeants.

At the trial, which opened on 21 August 1822 and lasted

two weeks, Bories declared his responsibility for the entire conspiracy in an attempt to save not only his comrades, but to avoid compromising the cause in which he so ardently believed. But despite his efforts and those of the defending council, he and three others, Pommier, Raoulx and Goubin, 'The Four Sergeants of La Rochelle' as they became known, were sentenced to death, the rest of the conspirators receiving less severe sentences.

After the verdict Bories handed a jewel to his lawyer and instructed him to give it to a person whose name has never been discovered. Then he, with his comrades, was taken to prison to await the end.

Three of those condemned to death appealed against the sentence, but on hearing that their leader Bories did not intend to avail himself of this last chance to avoid the scaffold, all withdrew their applications. The secret society responsible for their treachery attempted to bribe the governor of their prison to allow them to escape, but the governor's uncle, a priest, betrayed the plan to the authorities and so the last loophole was closed.

On 21 September Henri Sanson and his son attended the Conciergerie for the routine preparation of their prisoners. Resigned but still spirited, they submitted to the toilette. Raoulx was the most cheerful; alluding to his own lack of inches, he joked, 'Poor me – how much will remain of me when my head is gone?!'

The departure for the scaffold had been scheduled for four o'clock, but the Council of Ministers was still debating whether a reprieve should be granted. The King, Louis XVIII, was said to be in favour, his brother and most of the others were not. Meanwhile efforts were being made to persuade the four sergeants to divulge all they knew about the planned assassinations, but they refused, declaring that they preferred death before dishonour.

At five o'clock Henri was instructed to drive the loaded tumbrils to the execution site, the Place de Grève. There the sergeants refused to listen to the appeals of the priest to repent; mounting the scaffold Raoulx, being the youngest, was the first to be bound to the bascule, crying, '*Vive la liberté!*' as the plank was pivoted.

He was followed in turn by Goubin and Pommier, each

giving the same clarion call. The last sergeant, Bories, stepped forward. As he did so, he faced the crowd and proclaimed, 'Today you are silent, but a time shall come when you will repeat my last cry of "*Vive la liberté!*".' Next moment he had been strapped to the bascule, and Henri gave the order for the release of the blade.

Bories's words were prophetic, for eight years later the French people did indeed overthrow the Bourbon rulers; alas too late for the Four Sergeants of La Rochelle.

The identity of the recipient of Bories's jewel remained a secret, but thirty years later Henri-Clement, who had been present with his father at the trial and executions, described how over the years he had seen a woman, at first young, then turning prematurely old, go each morning to the Montparnasse cemetery and place a flower on her sweetheart's grave, a daily pilgrimage of love.

During the next few years Henri and his son supervised the operations on the scaffold together, the older man being nominally in charge of the assistants who actually carried out the punishments. The accounts of these, as seen through the eyes of young Henri-Clement, are included in the next chapter, but one gory instance took place on 28 October 1828, when father and son had to execute two women at Versailles. One had killed her husband, the other, Catherine Darcy, had murdered her mother.

Just as in the killing of a king, so he or she who murdered a parent suffered the loss of a hand before being executed, and this was the terrible sentence passed on Catherine Darcy. Henri-Clement's account reveals a hitherto unsuspected facet of his father's nature when he wrote: 'For this complication of capital punishment, my father had invented a contrivance by which the fist was so compressed that the pain was considerably diminished. Catherine Darcy however uttered fearful shrieks when her hand was severed, her cries only subsiding when the knife of the guillotine came down on her neck.'

It is regrettable that no description of the 'contrivance' has survived; possibly it was an arrangement by which the hand and arm were secured to a board, the straps then being tightened like a tourniquet so that the flow of blood was restricted sufficiently to deaden all feeling in the limb.

It was in 1832 that Henri must have wondered whether he was destined to be the last of the Sanson executioners, for after much public debate the Chamber of Deputies voted to abolish capital punishment, and although the Upper House refused its support for the motion, a law was passed on 28 April 1832 reducing the severity of punishments in general. Not only was the use of the pillory and branding iron abolished, but extenuating circumstances were to be taken into consideration in crimes which carried the death sentence.

As a consequence, widespread redundancies in the ranks

of French headsmen were announced, their numbers being reduced from eighty-six to about twenty. One can but feel sorry for those of the Sanson families operating in the provinces, many of whom lost their jobs, with little or no prospect of being accepted into any other profession. However, the post of Monsieur de Paris remained inviolate and intact.

By now Henri was in his sixties. A visitor to his home, Benjamin Appert, member of the Royal Society of French Prisons, described how, on entering the house, Henri rose from his chair and took off the white cotton bonnet he wore, revealing his large, bald head. Old execution swords lay on tables, and when Appert visited again he brought friends along, to whom Henri demonstrated the operation of the guillotine, escorting them to the shed where the device was stored. Greatly interested, they wanted to see it in action, and Henri obliged, the 15 lb. blade with its 65 lb. bronze weight dropping to cleave trusses of straw, no volunteers among the visitors being forthcoming!

Other contemporaries described him as a fine looking man, nearly six feet tall, with a gentle though pale face and an unmistakable patriarchal air about him as he elegantly took a pinch from his snuffbox.

At the age of sixty-nine Henri retired to the comfort of his home, leaving Henri-Clement in sole charge of the scaffold. Little is known of his few remaining years, but he passed away in August 1840. His wife Marie-Louise survived him until 1866, when she died, aged ninety. Her qualities as wife and mother were reflected in the inscription carved on the Sanson grave-stone; 'Rest in peace, worthy and loving mother. You did nothing but good. May God reward you by your acts.'

10   Henri-Clement: Last of the Line

If the profession of the Sansons could ever be classed as an honourable one, shame eventually blighted it with the birth of Henri-Clement. From Charles Sanson the first and the second, through Jean-Baptiste, Charles-Henri, to Henri, there was never a hint in their characters of anything other than integrity and absolute respectability. However, the boy who was born to Henri and Marie-Louise in 1799 was to be the exception to the rule.

His parents, and indeed his grandmother, were strongly opposed to the accepted idea that he should follow the family tradition when he grew up, and it was only because his grandfather, Charles-Henri, held the firm belief that, like a king, an executioner could not abdicate, that Henri-Clement subsequently took on the mantle, bloodstained though it was. Like any mother, Marie-Louise gave him his earliest education, and this was continued by an elderly abbé, a kind and learned gentleman who taught him his catechism, together with some basic education.

During those first few years the young boy was deliberately kept in ignorance of his father's work, and to this end he went to live with his grandparents at Brie-Comte-Robert. But when Charles-Henri died, the house was sold and Henri bought a country villa at Brunoy, a few miles from Paris, into which Marie-Anne, Charles-Henri's widow, moved. To shield his son further from the raw realities of what awaited him in adulthood, Henri not only purchased the property in the name of Longval rather than Sanson, but also arranged for the boy to live there with his grandmother.

Henri-Clement may have gleaned an inkling of his future after overhearing a conversation between his parents shortly after Charles-Henri's funeral, for he heard his father say

> My father was right; it's of no use to try and get out of the
> groove. Henri-Clement would always be reminded of his
> origin by his more fortunate friends, and would be more
> unhappy in society than out of it. I don't want my son to
> blush for his father. Let him get as good an education as
> money can procure, but let him remain the son of Messieurs
> de Paris and be true to his origin.

The boy heard his mother raise some objections, but his
father continued

> What profession could he possibly adopt? Everybody would
> spurn him. There is no law to prevent him entering some
> liberal profession; but the laws of society are more pitiless
> than those of the State. Were he a barrister, no one would
> ever consent to employ the services of an executioner's son,
> and it would be the same in every other direction. Believe
> me, we are providing for the best, and he will thank us
> afterwards for not making a 'gentleman' out of him.

Henri-Clement later commented that the words would
have made a deeper impression on him, had he been older at
the time; as it was, he received an intuitive impression of
what destiny had in store for him.

A local school was chosen in Brunoy, and there he enjoyed
himself, learning, with other subjects, music and drawing,
for which he found he had a natural bent. At the age of
twelve he returned to live with his parents in Paris, and it
was here that his halcyon days of innocence were due to end.
Henri had discussed his possible enrolment in the Institution
Michel with the headmaster who, after some hesitation, had
agreed to accept the boy as a pupil but diplomatically
suggested that he continue to be known under the name of
Longval.

All went well and Henri-Clement settled in happily, until
one day he invited a close school-friend of his to accompany
him home and meet his parents. They treated the lad with
some coldness, and it was not until Henri-Clement went to
school the following day that he found himself ignored, not

only by his friend, but also by all the other boys. None of them would speak to him, and it was not until he tackled his erstwhile friend that the boy drew something on a piece of paper and handed it to Henri-Clement. It was a rough sketch consisting of two upright beams, at the top of which was a large knife. Below, a man was strapped to a plank, while nearby stood another man holding the rope. And beneath the sketch his friend had printed '*TUUS PATER CARNIFEX*' (Your father is an executioner).

The revelation had an appalling effect on the 14-year-old boy; distraught, he rushed home and fainted in his mother's arms. The truth then had to be revealed, and Henri, taking his son aside, recounted the family history, emphasizing the inevitability of the Sanson way of life and telling him of his grandfather's dying wish; and that what had occurred at school was just an example of what would happen, should he choose another career. At length Henri-Clement accepted this with sad resignation, though later he admitted that at the time, being young and obedient to his father's reasoning, he had had little alternative.

School of course was now out of the question and Henri-Clement had to continue his education by his own efforts. Intelligent and willing to learn, he became proficient at the piano, and studied art, becoming quite an expert on paintings. At home he spent long hours browsing over the scores of rare books and manuscripts in the extensive family library, but the more philosophical and political works he read, the more mentally confused he grew over the role he was ultimately to fulfil in society. He accepted the argument that if capital punishment was justifiable, then surely the executioner was the most important functionary of the social order; yet such was his personal loathing for the death sentence that reconciliation of the two opposing factors became impossible.

In October 1817 his grandmother died and after the period of mourning he decided to spread his wings. He was eighteen, his imagination had been fired by his studies, and the world beckoned, a world that neither knew nor perhaps even cared what his name was. And so he travelled around Europe, to Italy and Germany, Holland and Switzerland, visiting art galleries and museums, libraries and churches.

After a year or more of such pleasurable wandering he returned to Paris, his regret at having to conform once more to his restricted lifestyle being dispelled on meeting a certain young lady, named Virginie-Emilie Lefebure. And he fell in love.

She was not one of his limited social circle, and it can only be surmised that perhaps one or other of her parents may have had cause to visit Henri's medical practice. Whatever the reason, Henri-Clement's sentiments were clearly reciprocated by Virginie who, much to his delight and surprise, showed neither hesitation nor reluctance at the prospect of being the wife of an executioner. Her father, Jean-Baptiste Alexis Lefebure, a wealthy woollen merchant, raised no objections, and so the young couple – she was a year older than he – were married in the church of Saint Laurent and moved into a cosy apartment in the Sanson house.

Their union seemed ideal; his wife was as happy and kind as she was attractive, and all augered well for their future together, though always on the horizon lurked the grim prospect of having to change their identity to that of Monsieur and Madame de Paris.

This came about far sooner than they had expected, when Henri succumbed to an attack of pleurisy, making it necessary for his son to take over. It was then that Henri-Clement must have recalled a conversation he had had years ago with his grandmother. 'I shall never have the courage to guillotine a man,' he had exclaimed to her. 'You have no choice,' she had replied sadly. 'The sooner you get used to the scaffold, the better.'

He had of course attended executions with his father in the past, but had only been present on the sidelines; now however he was to be chief executioner, hopefully only temporarily. His first victim was a soldier of the Royal Guard, Pierre Charles Rodolphe Foulard, guilty of murdering two women in order to rob them of a watch and a pair of earrings. Henri-Clement confessed that the night before the execution was the worst in his life, almost as bad no doubt as that spent by Foulard.

The next morning he went to the Conciergerie with his team. There the prisoner, a tall handsome man the same age as himself was waiting, outwardly calm and composed. After the necessary preparations, the tumbril was boarded, the ungainly vehicle then rumbling its way through the streets.

Among the crowd that surrounded the scaffold was a sergeant of the Guard who insisted on embracing the doomed man. Foulard then turned to Henri-Clement and exclaimed emotionally, 'Let me embrace you too, if only to show that I forgive everybody!'

An announcement like this would no doubt have shaken even the professional composure of Charles-Henri himself; to the 20-year-old youth supervising his first execution, it came as a shock such as he had never imagined. He stepped back and, as he admitted later, 'It was a fearful blow; I really think that if the unfortunate man had embraced me I could not have given the signal for his death.'

Fortunately for the state of his nerves, this was not necessary for, having previously been briefed by Henri, Fauconnier, the chief assistant, and his men understood Henri-Clement's instinctive recoil. Immediately they took over, pushing Foulard up the steps and binding him to the bascule; next moment the new Monsieur de Paris found himself looking at the bloody scene as one assistant rolled the headless body into a basket while another sponged the blood which had gushed over the boards; it was done.

In his memoirs Henri-Clement recalled that traumatic turning point in his life, when his destiny suddenly became stark reality. He wrote

> I was seized with irresistible horror and I ran away as fast as my legs could carry me. I wandered about the town hardly knowing what I was about. I thought people were following and hooting me. It was only when I found myself at Neuilly, some distance away, that I recovered, and even then my conscience smote me bitterly. At last I made up my mind. I had crossed the line, there was no help for it. I had, as it were, passed my examination of executioner, and I could not return on my steps. I went home subdued, if not comforted, and I found some relief in the thought that the first step was made, and the first bitterness had passed.

Once his initiation had been achieved, Henri-Clement's

nerves steadied and, although he never lost his natural disgust for his task, he controlled his emotions to a much greater extent during his subsequent appearances on the scaffold.

From then on he was to get much practice, for when, within weeks, Henri *père* regained his health, father and son worked together. During that year, 1819, parricide Moroy was beheaded, as was Liebe, a murderer. In May of the following year Charles Normand met his death for the slaying of his master, Captain Sion.

Soon after, Pierre Louvel, a 36-year-old saddler, was guillotined for killing the heir to the elder branch of the Bourbon family, the Duc de Berri, despite the duke's dying wish that his murderer should be pardoned. It was a cold, wet day and on boarding the tumbril Louvel, who was bald, calmly asked that he be allowed to wear his hat. Although this was contrary to the usual practice, for not only did headgear tend to obscure the victim's features from the crowd's view, but also wasted precious seconds on the scaffold, Henri-Clement kindly gave the required permission, and Fauconnier went back to the cell, retrieved the hat and, because the felon's hands were tied behind him, jammed it on his head for him.

Another milestone in Henri-Clement's working career occurred on 6 December 1820 when for the first time he watched a victim's hand being amputated. Pierre Louis Martin had murdered his father, and so the dire penalty was enacted, prior to decapitation.

Henri-Clement's marriage, initially promising so much, started to show signs of disharmony. Admittedly he and Virginie had had three children; the first, a boy, died in infancy in a carriage accident near Brunoy, a tragic event which inevitably brought grief to his parents. The circumstances of the accident are not known, but some would have attributed it to the hand of Fate, for had the infant not been killed, in all probability he would have become the seventh generation of Sanson executioners, with perhaps sons and grandsons to succeed him!

In 1818 Marie-Emilie was born; in 1843, she was to marry Jean-Nicolas Jouenne who, though a surgeon, was still 'within the trade', being a son and grandson of the executioners of Melun! After the marriage, the surprise expressed by a visitor at the profession of the groom, brought a witty response from Henri-Clement. 'Let us look at things from rather a higher standpoint,' he said. 'To save a human body a surgeon is often obliged to sacrifice an unhealthy member! So when one of the members of the social body is gangrened, is it not the right thing to sacrifice that also?' The visitor considered this for a moment, then exclaimed, 'Perhaps – but permit me to point out to you that there is a very great difference between the two sacrifices.' Henri-Clement smiled slowly. 'Yes, Monsieur,' he rejoined. 'In the size of the knife!'

The surgeon and the executioner's daughter raised a family, a girl, Marie-Henriette born in 1839, and a son, Paul-Louis, in 1841, both being doted on by their proud grandfather Henri-Clement.

Their second daughter, Thérèse Clementine Antoinette, was born in 1827 and she married Theodore-Joseph Clarisse, a clerk, in 1845. Few records exist of their life together, but it is known that Thérèse tended the Sanson family grave, placing flowers thereon each year, on the anniversary of the death of Louis XVI, 21 January. After the death of her husband, she retired to a convent where, the last of the line, she died in the early years of the twentieth century.

But much water was to pass under the bridge, and much blood flow from the scaffold, before all that happened. Through 1821 and 1822 the executions continued to be supervised by Henri and his son, though by degrees the latter played the major role. Murderers and thieves were duly dealt with, an unusual case being that of an arsonist, Louis Charlemagne Gosslin, who was found guilty of creating a reign of terror in the Oise *département* by setting fire to twenty-two houses in a single village.

Soon after came the trial and despatch of the Four Sergeants of La Rochelle, as recounted in the previous chapter. Then in 1823 Henri-Clement had the less gruesome task of supervising cases, not of execution, but exhibition, of criminals. This humiliation was only part of a sentence, the rest being that of imprisonment. One man who endured it was an escaped convict named Cognard who had somehow obtained the personal papers of the Comte de Saint-Hélène.

That aristocrat had died in Spain under suspicious circumstances and Cognard, bearing some resemblance to the dead man, assumed his identity, and returned to France, where he passed himself off as the comte. In his new guise he led a brilliant life and rose to the highest military ranks until, disastrously for him, he was identified and betrayed by a fellow convict. Unable to prove him guilty of murder, the court sentenced him to ten years hard labour, after being exhibited on the scaffold. He served all his punishment with extreme cynicism, and died sixteen years later in Toulon.

Another gentleman similarly shamed was General Jean Sarrasin. As in all cases of judicial exhibition, the victim's crimes were written on a placard which was prominently displayed to the crowd, and that prepared by Henri-Clement informed the spectators that the gallant officer had been found guilty of the truly heinous crime of polygamy! He had been foolhardy enough to marry no fewer than three times, once in Italy, once in England and once in France, and after an hour's humiliation he was taken away to serve ten years imprisonment.

On 6 December of the same year the young executioner – by then he was twenty-four years of age – guillotined the notorious criminal Edme-Samuel Castaing, a man whose execution taught Henri-Clement a great deal, not only about human nature but also about his own gullibility.

Castaing was a 27-year-old physician, believed to have been the first (known) murderer to kill by administering morphine. His victims were two intimate friends, brothers by the name of Ballet, and he persuaded them to bequeath all their property to him. After killing one, Castaing lured the other brother to a tavern, where he induced him to drink mulled wine, liberally dosed with morphine.

The murderer's hopes that the poison would not be detected were shattered when the pin-point condition of the dead man's eyes, indicating the presence of morphine, was observed by other doctors, and the authorities, their suspicions aroused by the terms of the wills, ordered a post-mortem. The result was a foregone conclusion and Castaing was tried and sentenced to death.

Accompanied this time by his father, Henri-Clement went to the prison to prepare their victim for his last journey.

Later he expressed his wonder that so black a soul could be concealed behind Castaing's soft and expressive face; the man was strikingly handsome, he said, and his blue eyes were devoid of any ferocious expression. When he saw the executioners he even shook a little, and pleaded, 'Pray do not harm me; you'll kill me ere long; until then it is of no use to make me suffer.'

While his hair was being cut, he referred to those he had murdered, exclaiming, 'Oh my dear friends, what would you say if you saw me in this sad position? I would have given my life to save you, and now I am charged with your death!'

Henri-Clement admitted that he himself was young and inexperienced, and it seemed impossible to him that a man could persist in such a terrible falsehood in the face of death. Castaing must have noticed the effect his words were having on the younger executioner, and when the assistant Fauconnier was about to tie his wrists he turned to Henri-Clement and pleaded, 'You bind my hands, sir, and do not draw the cords too tight!' Touched, Henri-Clement acquiesced, whereupon Castaing thanked him profusely.

En route in the tumbril he protested his innocence, shuddering when the scaffold came into view. Terror-stricken on arrival, he collapsed and had to be carried up the steps; on the platform he fell on his knees and, stretching out his hands to the Abbé Montes, he cried, 'Forgive me, father; I am guilty.'

After the guillotine had done its work, Henri-Clement admitted that he had been astounded by the man's duplicity; the suddenness of the murderer's confession had almost overcome him, and he realized that from that moment on, he would be more sceptical when his victims assured him of their innocence. In that respect Castaing did him a good turn, hardening Henri-Clement's more sensitive emotions and if not exactly making his task tolerable, at least easing his conscience.

Father and son continued their dual supervision as the years passed, Henri-Clement slowly taking full control, though Henri of course had to be present. In 1824 a mother and her son were guillotined for murder, the pair violently abusing each other all the way to the scaffold, much to the disgust of the Sansons. Three highwaymen, Ochard, Renaud and Delaporte, were similarly despatched, for waylaying stage coaches and robbing and killing their passengers.

The two executioners' tasks continued, albeit infrequently, only a few felons being guillotined each year. The case of the Abbé Joseph Contrafatto excited much public attention in 1828, the priest having been found guilty of a criminal attempt against a young girl. Henri-Clement described how the crowds hooted and abused the cleric as he was exhibited on the scaffold before being led away to endure seventeen years in the hulks, the dreaded prison ships which lay rotting in the harbours.

Such was the decline in scaffold traffic due to revised laws and the leniency of the courts, that in 1827 there were only eight executions, and none at all in Paris in 1831. One case in Versailles featured the validity or otherwise of phrenology and physiognomy, sciences much in fashion at that time, the first hypothesizing that the shape of a person's head determined their personality, the second claiming that those who LOOKED like criminals WERE criminals!

Robert Saint-Clair, an escaped convict and murderer, happened to be dining at a table already occupied by a group of friends, one of whom was a writer studying those now discredited sciences. Saint-Clair listened with scorn to the subject under discussion, interrupting to voice his contempt so much that the writer observed him closely, then said that, if permitted, he could describe the innermost nature of the disbeliever. Saint-Clair hesitated, then agreed; whereupon the writer said, 'Your features show the cunning of a fox and the ferocity of the wolf!'

Far from flattered, the convict sneered and remained silent until the end of the meal. Just as all were rising from the table, a number of gendarmes entered the room and asked the travellers to produce their passports for a routine check. Saint-Clair showed his and, despite it being in order, was identified and arrested. Found guilty of murder, he was taken to the scaffold and, whether the cause of his downfall was the shape of his head or not, it was removed by Henri-Clement and his chief assistant Piot.

Few executions took place in 1833 and the two following years. In 1836 Henri Sanson retired, his son taking over as Monsieur de Paris in everything but name. Within weeks he had his first important case to deal with, an outrage which united many royalists and republicans in condemnation of the perpetrators. On 28 July celebrations took place in the city to commemorate the Revolution of 1830, and the public turned out in full force to see the processions and join in the festivities. Security was minimal, despite the fact that on the previous day the police had been informed that an attempt was to be made on the life of the King.

In a third floor room of a house overlooking the route of the procession, a Corsican named Giuseppe Marco Fieschi had installed himself, together with an infernal machine which consisted of up to fifty rifles mounted on a wooden framework, their triggers being so connected that they could be fired simultaneously.

Fieschi, a thief, spy, forger and political murderer, had joined a revolutionary faction and with two other conspirators, Pepin and Morey, had hatched an assassination plot. As the royal cavalcade passed along the broad, densely packed boulevard, he fired his multiple gun. It detonated with a roar like thunder, the bullets spraying death and destruction among the spectators. The King himself escaped unharmed, though his horse was hit by a bullet, but there were many casualties, forty people being killed or seriously wounded, including a marshal of France and several generals and officials, scores of others receiving minor injuries.

For Fieschi there was no escape; the primitive device had either backfired or, more likely, not being bolted to the floor, had recoiled so violently that he had also been injured.

All three were sentenced to death and were escorted to the scaffold by Henri-Clement. It was a cold windy day and the executioner, despite his repugnance towards his victim, asked Fieschi, who was wearing only a vest and breeches, whether he would like a coat. The man sneered at him and, defiant to the end, exclaimed, 'No, I shall be a lot colder when they bury me!'

Because of the virtual massacre of innocent citizens, the crowds had turned out in their thousands to scream abuse at the murderous crew, and soldiers had been drawn up to cordon off the immediate area. Nevertheless the executioner and his team were apprehensive and wasted little time in hustling their victims up the steps.

First to be guillotined was Theodore-Florentin Pepin, a withered old man, and under other circumstances Henri-Clement could have felt sorry for him. As it was, he commented that at least the man died with dignity. Then followed Morey, a man in his thirties, with four young children; he also was brave to the last. As for Fieschi, Henri-Clement said contemptuously that the would-be assassin fainted away while his assistants were strapping him to the plank.

By now the frenzied mob was crushing against the rails, bent on seizing souvenirs of the murderers, even perhaps on carrying away the bodies in triumph. With mounting alarm Henri-Clement gathered up any garments that came to hand, even pieces of the cords which had bound the felons' hands, and threw them to the plundering mob, as if fending off sharks; then desperately he and his men moved the bodies into the carts and, protected by the gendarmerie, made their escape.

This experience, together with his innate revulsion for his work, exacerbated Henri-Clement's already dissolute lifestyle. Home life held little or no appeal for him, and he had neither the inclination nor the need to practise medicine as had his father and grandfather; for one thing he saw too much blood on the scaffold to want to treat patients, and he had no need for extra income, the family wealth being more than sufficient.

If he had to be an executioner, he reasoned, he'd spend the rest of his life doing what HE wanted, and so, whether just weak by nature or in sheer defiance of the horrors he faced on the scaffold, he lived the life of a fashionably dressed man about town, drinking heavily and becoming a *habitué* of fashionable gambling houses and the city's race course. He haunted artists' studios, bought expensive paintings, and visited houses of ill-repute, his constant absences from home threatening to wreck his already precarious marriage.

On the scaffold he left most of the work to his chief assistant Piot, but whether active or merely supervising, the sight and sounds of the decapitations brought him out in a nervous rash. 'No one was more distraught than I, when I received my orders for an execution; I became quite feverish,' he admitted in later years.

On 18 August 1840 his father died, and on 1 December of that year Henri-Clement was officially appointed Monsieur de Paris. At that time he lived in a little house in the rue des Marais Saint Martin, that was unobtrusive in appearance but very comfortable. His assistants lived in the house and acted as his servants. Retired executioners from the provinces also liked to live with him when they settled in Paris, finding it easier to hide their past there than in the districts where they were known, and in order to secure through his good offices the pensions or yearly allowances allotted to them by the Minister of Justice.

Executions during the next seven years were few, only eighteen taking place by 1847. One, which occurred on 30 November 1843, was that of Henri Salmon, condemned to death for murdering a man in the Vincennes forest. Following his usual practice of leaving everything to Piot, Henri-Clement was surprised when his assistant reported that Salmon wished the executioner to superintend the toilette in person, saying that he knew the Sanson family, and adding that he hoped Henri-Clement would spare him as much pain as possible. Touched somewhat by this appeal, the executioner agreed, doing what he could to ease the man's death.

But sentimental instances like that were rare. The next execution, on 27 January 1844, saw the appearance of Poulman, alias Durand, alias Legrand, on the scaffold, for the murder of the owner of a wine-shop. Henri-Clement described how, when the hour of punishment came, Poulman showed the most extraordinary courage.

The felon was particularly proud of his strength [the executioner wrote in his memoirs] and as it was feared that he would try and make a show of it before dying, I deemed it advisable to double the number of my assistants. These apprehensions were groundless, although when my assistants advanced to secure his hands behind him, Poulman looked up angrily and asked whether it was the custom. 'Because if it is not,' he growled, 'I'll send you all tumbling over in less than a minute!' However, he submitted, but would not allow the Abbé Montes to accompany him.

When we reached the scaffold Poulman looked at the

guillotine without as much as a shudder. 'Is that all?' he exclaimed, shrugging his shoulders. On reaching the platform he turned to my assistants and asked, 'I say, you fellows, won't you put a franc in my pocket for the grave-diggers? It is bitterly cold, and the poor fellows must drink my health!' And with those words, he submitted to the knife.

By now, Henri-Clement had fallen seriously into debt. Driven by the need both to stave off those dunning him, and the desire to continue his debauched and profligate way of life, he had no alternative but to sell the family shares, the expensive furniture, even his precious paintings. But so pressing were his creditors, so reduced his capital, that eventually the debtors' prison loomed.

This institution, situated on the rue de Clichy, was of a peculiar nature. It housed no murderers, no criminals; it had neither cells nor warders as such. No hardship was involved; on the contrary, the private rooms were warm and clean, facilities such as a library, a restaurant, a games area and even a post office, being available. The 'Clichy' as it became known, was more of a gentlemen's club for those who, to put it delicately, were in constrained financial circumstances. Confinement therein carried no stigma or disgrace, even the shame of arrest being avoided, since the debtor was escorted there, not by gendarmes, but discreetly by *recors*, bailiffs' men.

Nor were the inmates imprisoned for twenty-four hours a day, but were free to leave whenever they wished. Should they do so, however, they were then liable to be sought after by the *recors*, who would escort them back to the Clichy. But the rules were so framed that the *recors* only had the authority to seize their victims during daylight hours, between six a.m. and six p.m.; moreover the *recors* had no powers at all outside the city boundaries.

When therefore a debtor realized that his creditors were closing in on him and that his name was on the bailiffs' list, he would spend convivial days out with similarly impecunious companions in the more fashionable villages in the countryside, returning to wait at the city gates until six o'clock. After a night with his family – or carousing, for no one ever spent their very last franc! – he would depart before dawn, a fugitive again, until nightfall.

It was of this company that Henri-Clement, hunted by his principal creditors, became a member, scuttling out of town in the early hours, creeping back home in the evening; and over his head all the time swung the sword of Damocles in the shape of the public prosecutor who, literally at any moment, might suddenly demand his presence on the scaffold – in the daytime!

Infrequent as executions were becoming, Henri-Clement knew that the respite could not possibly last forever; nor did it, for in April 1846 another attempt on the lives of the royal family was made.

It happened as the King and Queen, accompanied by their grandchildren, were travelling in an open carriage through the forest of Fontainebleau about six o'clock in the evening. Suddenly two shots rang out from the top of a wall bordering an enclosure. Instantly the grooms and outriders gave chase, and captured a man whose face was concealed beneath a handkerchief. Fortunately the royal passengers were uninjured, and the man was taken into custody.

The would-be assassin was Pierre Lecomte, the head ranger of the forest who had recently been disciplined and fined for ill-treating members of his staff. Incensed by the penalty he had resigned, demanding a pension for his length of service. His frustration grew when his claim was rejected, and he refused to accept the explanation that he was ineligible, being merely an employee in a private forest owned by the King rather than a civil servant. Appeals to Louis-Philippe failing, in desperation he resorted to the action which could have but one result in the court before which he appeared; the death sentence.

For Henri-Clement, too, the game was up; the death sentence passed on Pierre Lecomte would also bring in its wake a prison sentence for the executioner.

On 8 June 1846 the small convoy of carts transporting Lecomte, the abbé, the executioner and his staff from the Conciergerie to the scaffold site was one vehicle longer than usual. The extra one was a carriage, and as Henri-Clement eyed it closely, he realized with sinking heart that the sole passenger was a process server who, not unlike the executioner himself, was coming in for the kill, albeit less painfully.

The *recors*, a patient man who knew that his prey was as good as in his grasp, bided his time. Ordering the coachman to park within sight of the scaffold, he watched the gory proceedings; the fall of the blade, the depositing of body and head in the basket, and the loading of the remains into the cart under the now nervous supervision of Henri-Clement. He then directed the coachman to accompany the cart, at a discreet distance, on its journey to the cemetery. And as Sanson returned to his house, looking over his shoulder the while, the *recors* intercepted him and duly served the necessary process.

That night, and for many of the following days and nights, Henri-Clement found himself confined to the Clichy, a state of affairs which, contrasting as harshly as it did with his usual roistering existence, rapidly proved unbearable. But what could he do? Besieged by his creditors, bereft of cash, his assets realized, his capital squandered; the outlook was bleak indeed. And then he had a brainwave – why not offer his chief creditor a really valuable article as collateral, something which would guarantee his freedom from this infernal prison for an indefinite period, something which even now was in his store-room, instantly available to be handed over – the guillotine! After all, with executions being so infrequent nowadays, it could be weeks, maybe months before it was required again, and that would give him ample time to recoup his losses on the gambling tables or the race track and redeem the machine.

Escorted by a *recors* Sanson visited his shed and, loading the guillotine into a horse-drawn van, he took it to the man to whom he owed the most money. The creditor no doubt was momentarily taken aback, but eventually accepted the device as security, assuring Henri-Clement that he would release it back into the executioner's possession on being paid the 3,800 francs he was owed.

Free at last, Sanson returned to his old haunts and, while not really making much effort to accumulate sufficient funds with which to regain his property, concentrated on enjoying himself in the style to which he had been accustomed. Occasionally he found himself studying the newspapers, or listening to conversations in bars for any mention of wanted criminals being captured, for deep within he knew he was living on borrowed time. And so he was, for on 17 March 1847, he was ordered to report to the Palais de Justice to collect and execute a condemned man on the following day. Panicking, he rushed to the creditor, pleading for the loan of his device, if only for the one day, but the man was adamant; no 3,800 francs, no guillotine.

It was a fearful Henri-Clement who reported to the Minister of Justice later the same day, and that gentleman's reactions on being faced by an executioner who had pawned his guillotine would beggar all powers of description. Suffice it to say that when the incredulous official had, with a superhuman effort, regained some semblance of his normal composure, he advanced Sanson the required sum with which to retrieve the essential machine. This was duly done, and the execution took place on schedule.

And on 18 March 1847 Henri-Clement, Executioner of High Justice, Monsieur de Paris, responsible for having decapitated 111 criminals during his career on the scaffold, was sacked!

Nor was this peremptory dismissal the only blow to Sanson's pride, for within weeks his wife, Virginie-Emilie, disillusioned by the empty and unhappy life she had been forced to accept, left him and went to live with her daughter Marie-Emilie and her surgeon husband Jean-Nicolas Jouenne in Versailles.

Henri-Clement, discredited and in debt, out of work at the age of forty-eight, his Paris house and the Brunoy villa sold to defray his overwhelming expenses and repay his creditors, had little option but to vanish into obscurity. With his ageing mother Marie-Louise, he adopted an assumed name and moved into a small village somewhere in the countryside where he proceeded to write his *Memoirs*, first published in 1862.

Three years after his dismissal his mother died, and in 1857 Henri-Clement moved to a village on the outskirts of Paris. There he was able to renew old friendships, one acquaintance, Georges Grison, describing him at the time in the newspaper *Le Figaro*, as: 'a little, fat, clean-shaven man, with the head of a Rabelaisian monk, and a chin shining with the cold cream he rubbed on it five or six times a day, no one knew why!'

After the death of his wife in March 1860 however, he too moved to Versailles and lived with his eldest daughter, who cared for him until, on 25 January 1889, he died aged eighty-nine and was buried in Montmartre cemetery.

And so, after dominating the Paris scaffold for 159 years, six generations of the Sanson dynasty of executioners finally came to an end. But lest it be thought that the repugnance felt towards such a vile occupation was universal, it must be pointed out that when the vacancy was advertised, no fewer than fifty applicants responded to the blandishments of 'Madame Guillotine'!

Appendix A
Paris Executions

Table summarizing the executions which took place in Paris during the revolutionary period 14 July 1789 to 21 October 1796

Age of the Executed	Number
Under 18 years	22
18–20 years	45
20–25 years	336
25–50 years	1669
50–60 years	528
60–70 years	206
70–80 years	103
Above 80 years	9
Men	2548
Women	370
Total	2918

Profession and Social Position of the Executed	Number
Members of the Church, Bishops and Archbishops	6
Marshals of France and Lieutenant-Generals	25
Magistrates, members of the ancient Parliaments	246
Ecclesiastics, priests, monks, etc.	319
Members of the Constituent and Legislative Assemblies	39
Members of the Convention	45
Members of the Commune	72
Liberal professions, financiers, barristers, doctors, lawyers, functionaries	479
Gentlefolk of both sexes without profession	381
Officers and soldiers	365
Writers and journalists of both sexes	275
Artists	16
Tradesmen of both sexes	25
Artisans	391
Servants of both sexes	129
Labourers and peasants	105
Total	**2918**

Appendix B
Living Though Beheaded?

The guillotine blade descends – the head is severed – the victim is dead. Or is he? Exactly WHEN did consciousness slip away? The very millisecond that the knife sliced through tissue, flesh and muscle, cleaving his spinal cord? Or was there sufficient blood still flowing within his brain to maintain some residue of life force to enable him, if only for an infinitesimal length of time, to hear the exultant roar of the crowd, to see the basket coming up to meet him? Or maybe even long enough, as his head was held on high, to look down at the gloating faces in the crowd as they gazed up in triumph?

This awful possibility has engaged the minds and brains of many renowned doctors and professors over the centuries, and here I am greatly indebted to Dr Harold Hillman, Reader in Physiology, Director of Applied Neurobiology at the University of Surrey, who provided much invaluable information on the subject.

It is known that, after a person or animal has been killed, surgically removed organs go on functioning; a transplanted heart can continue to beat, a moistened kidney continue to produce urine, even a cow's udder will still produce milk. Chemical processes resulting in the production of energy continue in slices of brain, liver or kidney; one can homogenize tissue and separate a mitochondrial fraction, which takes up oxygen for hours; so can all these organs be classed as dead? And if, in that context, they are alive, can the brain itself, in a severed head, survive for an unknown number of seconds; and if it IS alive, is its owner conscious?

After having been decapitated, the eyes of small rodents

move for some seconds; dogs are conscious for up to twelve seconds after blood supply to the brain has been stopped, and it has been calculated that as far as human beings are concerned, there is sufficient oxygen stored in the brain to persist for about seven seconds, further energy being derived from the layers of tissue in the scalp and the facial and neck muscles, though it is considered that consciousness itself is probably lost within two to three seconds after severance.

Throughout history there have been accounts of life apparently continuing after decapitation. Anne Boleyn, beheaded by the sword in the Tower of London, was seen to move her eyes and lips for many moments afterwards, though this, like the twitching of headless animals, could be attributed solely to muscular reactions. During the French Revolution many thousands of people witnessed the guillotine in action over the years, scores of spectators swearing that when François le Gros held Charlotte Corday's severed head and smacked its cheek, the other cheek also blushed, as if with indignation.

Professor of medicine Pierre Sue confirmed this, stating:

> The face of the victim, which until then had been pale, had no sooner received the slap, than both cheeks blushed visibly. All the spectators observed the change in colour and immediately raised their voices and demanded restitution for this cowardly and atrocious act of barbarity.
>
> One could not say that this redness was the effect of the slap, for when the cheeks of a corpse are struck, immediately after death, they never change colour. Moreover this slap was given on only one cheek, whereas it was seen that the other cheek also blushed. This fact alone proves conclusively that after decapitation there is still a little judgement remaining in the brain, and a trace of sensibility in the nerves.

As always in such cases, voices were raised to the contrary. A Dr Leveillee protested volubly:

> So the face of Charlotte Corday blushed? I don't believe it for a minute. I am prepared to admit the possibility of this reddening, but when I look for the cause, it is purely

mechanical. In fact this head still retained not necessarily its vital force, but certainly its vital warmth; the blood still fluid in the small capillary vessels, flowed freely when its course was suddenly interrupted by the violent blow from le Gros's hand.

This revolting action brought the walls of the vessels together, and the blood coming from the upper part was unable to pass below the constricted spot, so it collected in sufficient quantity to produce the reddening which M. Sue, falsely, in my opinion, attributes to a vestige of judgement and sensibility. But when he says that the other cheek also blushed, well, that is really pushing observation too far, and I really cannot believe it.

Jules Michelet, in a history of the French Revolution published in 1878, put forward yet another hypothesis when he wrote:

At the moment the head fell, a carpenter on the scaffold grabbed it violently, showed it to the people and had the outrageous savagery to slap it. A shudder of horror and murmurs of disapproval ran round the square. People thought they saw the head blush. Probably an optical illusion; the crowd, disturbed at that moment, had the red rays of the sun which shone through the trees of the Champs-Elysées in their eyes.

Little actual credence can be given to M. Michelet's theory, as he was not even alive at the time. For the same reason, the explanation presented by M. Chevron Villiers, biographer of Charlotte Corday, can similarly be discounted when he wrote; 'The executioner's hands were covered with blood and so left their mark on the cheeks of the dead woman.'

An eye-witness, M. Duval, threw doubt on the occurrence altogether, though was diplomatic enough not to be too unequivocal about it, saying:

I, who was at the entrance to the Champs-Elysées and therefore quite close to the scaffold, did not see it. Let me say at once that I do not dispute the fact; I simply say that I did not see it. I must add that one of my neighbours did not see it either, and it was not until several days later that I heard this rumour circulating in Paris.

The Marquise de Crequy, an erudite lady who survived the Revolution, mentioned the incident in her *Souvenirs*, published in 1836, going on to report experiments which had been carried out. She had asked a Dr Seguret, professor of anatomy, whether Charlotte Corday could really have been aware of the slap, continuing:

> He assured us that such a thing was possible, and told us that he had been asked to conduct experiments on the effects of the guillotine, and that he had had delivered to him the remains of several criminals immediately after their deaths, and that he had observed the following results.
>
> He said, 'We exposed two heads to the sun's rays and we opened the eyelids. The eyelids promptly closed of their own accord, and with an alertness that was both abrupt and startling. The entire face then assumed an expression of intense suffering.
>
> 'The mouth of one of these heads was open, with its tongue protruding. A student decided to prick the tongue with the point of a lancet, whereupon it withdrew into the mouth and its features grimaced as if in pain.
>
> 'Another of the guillotine's victims, an assassin called Terier, was subjected to similar tests, and more than a quarter of an hour after decapitation, his eyes turned in the direction of the man who was speaking.'
>
> 'The guillotine is one of the most horrible and most inhuman kinds of death invented by man,' the doctor continued. 'The agony that follows beheading is excruciating, and I firmly believe that it continues until all heat has left the body. This philanthropic invention is easy to operate, advantageous to the French Republic and above all, convenient for the executioner, but no one can say that it is advantageous or convenient to the victim, because it is certain that strangulation cannot be as painful.'

It is certainly likely that the victim could experience severe pain due to the stretching of the skin prior to severance, and then a burning sensation and intense agony on laceration, but if consciousness DOES continue for any length of time after decapitation, the pain may be intense enough to speed complete oblivion.

In 1795 the results of experiments carried out by an anatomist, Dr Sommering, were published which convinced him that life did continue for some short time after decapitation. He quoted cases where a head had grimaced as if in pain when a finger was inserted into the spinal canal, and where severed heads had been heard to grind their teeth!

The whole problem was of course that, the vocal cords having been cut by the guillotine knife, there was no method of communication between head and experimenter. What was needed was to decide on some sort of a code with a condemned man, someone so dedicated to the cause of aiding humanity at the moment of his own sacrifice that he would co-operate in imparting the necessary information by answering the questions put to him with pre-arranged winks, lip movements and changes in expression.

But taking all the circumstances into consideration this was highly unlikely, to say the least. Criminals being guillotined would hardly be committed to such a philanthropic motive. Even if they were, would their brain remember what to do at such a terrible moment; if it did, would the necessary thought sequence not be overwhelmed by the intensity of their agonies?

The controversy continued to stimulate debate on humanitarian and anatomical grounds long after the echoes of the Revolution had died away. In 1905 reports of experiments carried out on the murderer Languille were included in publications specializing in criminal anthropology. The researcher, Dr Beaurieux, present at the execution, described how; 'The head fell on the severed surface of the neck and I did not therefore have to take it up in my hands; I was not even obliged to touch it in order to set it upright.' (This would seem hard to visualize, as a victim lies prone, with his head over the basket. Perhaps the executioner's assistant caught the head and replaced it on the neck, the body having been turned over and placed in a seated posture.)

The doctor's report continued

I noted that the eyelids and lips worked in irregular rhythmic contractions for about six seconds; I waited for several seconds, when the spasmodic movements ceased. The face relaxed, the lids half closed on the eyeballs, leaving only the white of the conjunctiva visible.

It was then that I called, 'Languille!' I then saw the eyelids slowly lift, without any jerky motion but just as one would on awaking from sleep; next Languille's eyes very definitely fixed themselves on mine and the pupils focussed themselves, not with a dull, blank look, but alert and concentrated. Then after several seconds the eyelids closed again, slowly and evenly.

Again I called out, and once more the eyelids opened and those undeniably living eyes fixed on mine; the eyelids closed again, slower this time, and although I called again, there was no response, the eyes having taken on the glazed look of the dead.

If, over the twenty-five to thirty seconds duration of the experiment, the auditory organs could stimulate the visual nerves into action, can we then assume that the upper part of the brain, that which controls consciousness, can also survive for some if not all of that time span?

Other researchers pursued different methods of investigation, one being reported in March 1907 in the publication *Le Matin*. It was carried out by Dr Dassy de Lignieres on a murderer named Menesclou. Although the man had been dead for some three hours, the doctor connected a blood supply from a living dog to the severed head. Within minutes the results were astonishing, for colour returned to the pale cheeks, the lips took on their normal shape and the face looked alive, as if the owner was about to speak! As the canine blood continued to flow, more developments took place, the lips twitching and the eyelids flickering. But this was all, and the scientific findings were inconclusive; the results could not be assumed to have regenerated the brain, but rather had done little more than mechanically trigger physical organs into movement, akin to pumping up a car tyre and observing the treads assuming their original shape.

Physiological deductions will no doubt continue to be made on the basis of known factors. Micro-surgery, the re-attachment of severed limbs, is now very successful, and hearts, livers, kidneys and other organs remain 'alive' long enough to function when required to be transplanted. So why should the brain not survive for a finite if unknown number of seconds? Unfortunately, like death itself, only those who personally experience decapitation know what happens – and within what time-scale.

Appendix C
French Torture Through the Ages

Amputation and Mutilation

There is scarcely a single part of the body that has not been subjected to a separate and special torture; the eyes, mouth, tongue, ears, teeth, arms, hands, feet and heart have all been sources of suffering by knife and fire.

The punishment of blinding, resorted to under the first two families of kings, was inflicted on high-born rivals whose lives they dared not take. This torture was inflicted on Bernard, King of Italy, grandson of Charlemagne, and in the year 873 the parliament of Senlis ordered that the rebellious son of Charles the Bald should be deprived of his sight.

There were various methods at the disposal of the torturer; a red-hot iron could be passed before the eyes until they were literally cooked; a sharp point could be plunged into the centre of the eyeball; or the eye itself could be plucked from its socket.

The tongue was always a favourite target, especially for those guilty of blasphemy. Louis IX ordered that such criminals should be branded on the brow, their lips burned, and their tongues pierced with a red-hot iron. For this he invented a cup-shaped iron which, after heating, would be pressed against the offender's lips. These penalties so terrified the nobles of the day that in order to escape the King's wrath, and at the same time placate the offended clerics, they moderated many of the oaths they used so that the expletives sounded almost the same but did not infringe the dreaded law. Thus *Tête de Dieu* (head of God) became *Tête bleu*, *Corps de Dieu* (body of God) became *Corbleu* and *Sang de Dieu* (blood of God) was changed to *Sang bleu*.

These modified oaths entered the language, their original forms eventually being forgotten, in the same way as, for example, in England the exclamation 'God blind me' became 'Corblimey' and, albeit less blasphemously, 'God be with ye' became 'goodbye'.

Louis XII enacted that whoever uttered eight blasphemies should have his tongue torn out, and this was re-enacted by his successor Louis XIV. One man who suffered this was Antoine Poile who, on 21 January 1535, had his tongue pierced and attached to his cheek with an iron pin, the tongue probably being pulled out of his mouth before being secured.

The amputation of the ear was widely employed in the Middle Ages, especially on serfs who disobeyed their masters. Laws enacted in 1498 and 1534 stated that 'the amputation of one ear [usually the left one] was to be inflicted on dishonest servants and cutpurses, a second offence to cost them the other ear; and the penalty for a third offence was death'.

The teeth were sometimes extracted, in a far from gentle manner, as a 'persuasive' measure to force Jews to give up their money. Louis IX, after having the Comte de Nemours executed, ordered that his children should be imprisoned in the Bastille, after first having their teeth extracted.

The amputation of the hand was the form of mutilation which resisted the progress of civilization for the longest time, until the Penal Code of 1791 enacted that 'whoever shall be condemned to death for murder or arson shall be taken to the place of execution clad in a red shirt. A parricide [one who murders a parent] shall have his head and face covered with a black cloth, which shall only be removed before execution'. But the Code of 1810 returned to the old primitive legislation which decreed that the hand of a parricide should first be amputated, and this edict was not cancelled until 1832.

The amputation of the feet was a wholly medieval punishment, the last recorded instance being in the reign of St Louis in the eighth century.

Boots

As its name implies, this torture was designed to inflict pain on the legs. There were differing designs, one consisting of four boards between which the victim's legs were pressed after the manner of splints. The boards were pierced with holes through which ropes were passed and tightened. The torturer then drove wedges between the planks with a mallet, compressing and eventually shattering the limbs. The *question ordinaire*, requiring admission of guilt for the crime committed, involved four wedges, these being driven between the two inner boards. Following the confession of guilt the *question extraordinaire* would be put, calling for the names of confederates, any reluctance being overcome by the forced insertion of four more wedges, this time between the outer boards and the victim's legs. It was usually effective.

Another version incorporated a screw mechanism which had the same, albeit excruciatingly slower result. Other types of boot, similar to iron wellingtons, were forced on the victim's feet and then held over a fire while the questions were put.

Bridle

Designed mainly to curb a nagging woman's tongue, this consisted of an iron cage which was locked about her head. The framework incorporated eye holes and an aperture for the mouth. At the front, protruding inwards, was a flat plate which was inserted into her mouth, there to rest firmly on her tongue and so foil any further attempt at speech. In some versions the tongue plate was studded with sharp pins or, even more painful, was replaced by a rowel, a small spiked wheel. An attached chain permitted the culprit to be led through the streets, to receive the attention of her neighbours. Lest they should be indoors at the time, some bridles incorporated a spring-mounted bell on top to signal her approach.

Collar

Known as the *carcan*, this was an iron collar which was riveted about the offender's neck, he or she then being led through town behind the executioner's cart, hands tied behind their back. At the place designated, usually the market cross or town whipping-post, the victim would be secured by having another iron collar six inches wide padlocked about the neck, this being attached to the post by means of a long chain. A placard detailing the crime would also be prominently displayed nearby.

Ducking Stool

Again, a measure whereby the victim was shamed rather than injured. Many towns and villages were adjacent to rivers or streams, others having their own duck pond (was the derivation of the word, at least in England, based on the bird which inhabited it, or the punitive use to which it was put? Was the word originally a 'ducking pond'?). An offender against the community was strapped into a wooden chair (sometimes ominously called a tumbril), then thoroughly doused in the water a specified number of times. Depending on circumstances, the chair would either be lowered from a bridge, or suspended from a long beam which, by being hinged centrally, would lower the chair into the depths.

Estrapade

Also known as *squassation*, this torture, invented in the sixteenth century during the reign of Francis I, involved the culprit falling from a height in such a manner as to break his limbs. The victim's hands would be tied behind his, or her back, a rope from the cord passing over a pulley in the roof beams. Thus hoisted off the ground, then allowed to drop abruptly, usually resulted in at least dislocation of the shoulder-blades.

Ladder

Similar in operation to the rack, this consisted of a wide ladder secured to the wall at an angle of forty-five degress. The victim was positioned on his back part-way up, wrists being tied to a rung behind him. A rope about his ankles was then passed round a pulley or roller at the foot of the ladder which, when pulled, would draw the victim down the ladder, wrenching his arms up behind him and causing severe pain to his arms and shoulder-blades. Sometimes lighted candles would at the same time be applied to his armpits and sides, to induce a confession.

Ordeal by Fire

A commonly used torture, applied in many different ways. The victim could be bound in a spiked iron chair, a fire being stoked beneath the seat; pincers, heated in the fire, could be applied to various tender parts of the victim's body; branding of course was much used and has already been described

Ordeal by Boiling Water

A cauldron of water, heated until boiling, would then be removed from the fire; by means of a cord tied above it, a ring or similar object would be suspended in the water, its depth depending on the crime that had been committed. The minimum ordeal specified to obtain a confession entailed the victim having to plunge just his hand in to seize the ring; at the second ordeal, he would need to plunge his arm in up to the elbow, and for the maximum ordeal, the whole arm would have to be immersed in the boiling water. After the torture the culprit's arm would be inserted in a bag on which the judge had imprinted his seal. Three days later this would be removed and the arm closely inspected. Should any sign of scalding be visible, the victim was declared guilty, and only if no apparent injury had been caused was he considered innocent of the crime.

Ordeal of the Cross

Employed in France in the ninth century, this unusual but no doubt effective method consisted of attending church and, during divine service, holding one's arms out, cross-fashion, for as long as possible. He who retained this position for the greater length of time was considered to have beaten his opponent. In his will Charlemagne decreed that the judgement of the cross should be resorted to in all quarrels arising from the division of his estates between his children.

Pillory

Neck pillories, double pillories, cage pillories, all were utilized through the ages. The first device, a flat piece of wooden board with an appropriately sized opening, protruded some few inches in front of the miscreant and was locked about his or her neck for the designated number of hours. Unlike other types of pillory, it permitted full freedom of movement; nevertheless the wearer was obviously an object of shame until released by the executioner or sergeant at arms.

The double pillory was, as its name implies, worn by two people at the same time. They, usually two women guilty of excessive arguing with each other, were locked by their necks into the device, their faces being only inches apart. Sometimes a bowl of soup and a spoon would be provided, each woman having one hand freed; the need to use the same spoon and partake from the same bowl sometimes, but not always, bringing about reconciliation.

The cage pillory in Paris, as mentioned in the text, consisted of a chamber at the top of an octagonal tower in which the offenders were displayed to the public. The chamber, on a pivot, was rotated every half an hour or so, exhibiting the occupants to all sides; placards describing their misdeeds gave the reason for the punishment. Different towns had other methods; in Orléans for example a culprit was enclosed in a wooden cage six feet high by two and a half feet wide. This was also mounted on a pivot but, being at ground level, members of the public could rotate it, the better to hurl insults, or unsavoury missiles, at their target.

Rack

There were several versions of this device, although all of them were designed to stretch the victim and progressively dislocate the ankle and knee, hip, shoulder, elbow and wrist joints. In early models a rope about the victim's ankles was tightened by means of a capstan; some also included the shoulder-shattering *estrapade*, the wrists being bound behind the back instead of above the head. Later versions required the victim to be stretched horizontally on a wooden frame, ropes from wrists and ankles being wound around rollers which were then slowly rotated in opposite directions. In order to maintain the tension on the ropes while interrogation took place, a cog wheel and ratchet was incorporated on each roller, the terrifying clicking sound inflicting mental as well as physical torture on the prisoner. An additional refinement was sometimes employed, that of having one or more spiked rollers positioned under the victim's back, as a further inducement to loosen his tongue.

Screw-operated Headband

This device, a wide metal strap which encircled the head, could be tightened a fraction at a time, thereby applying unbearable agony to the nerve centres of the brain and, if overtightened, could eventually fracture the victim's skull.

Stocks

Similar to the English design, the stock required the miscreant to be seated, usually in or near the village green, with his or her feet stretched out before them, ankles being gripped in the apertures of two hinged boards padlocked together at one end. Painless but highly embarrassing, the occupant being the object of all eyes and insults.

Thumbscrews

Originally resembling primitive nutcrackers, these developed into deadly pieces of the torturer's equipment. Similar to a diminutive ox-yoke, the device consisted of two short iron bars of equal length, one having three small rods designed to slide into the three matching holes in the other bar.

The victim's fingers were inserted between the bars on each side of the central rod, which had a screw thread on it. Once positioned over the quick of the nails, the nut on the central rod was tightened, forcing the upper bar downwards and so applying a variable amount of pressure on the nails. Some models were designed to fit solely on to the thumb, others were dual, exerting unbearable pressure on the nails of both hands simultaneously.

Water Torture

For this horrific torture the victim was strapped immovable on a bench, the interrogator then inserting a horn into his or her mouth. For the *question ordinaire*, four pints of water were poured into the funnel, and double that quantity for the *question extraordinaire*. Any reluctance to swallow was overcome by the torturer pinching the victim's nose, and if by some phenomenal strength of mind the victim resisted, death could result from water eventually entering and flooding the lungs, causing death by asphyxiation.

Whipping

A standard method, frequently used, though mainly as a punishment rather than a torture. Stripped to the waist and either lashed behind the executioner's cart while traversing the streets, or with wrists secured to rings set in a wall, it provided considerable public entertainment especially when, regrettably, the offender was a woman.

Wooden Horse

This, the *cheval de bois*, was formed of planks nailed together to form a long ridge or angle, about eight or nine feet in length. The ridge represented the back of a horse, and it was usually supported by four posts or legs on a stand or wheeled

platform. Sometimes a replica head was added, together with a tail of horse-hair. The culprit, wrists tied behind him, would be made to straddle the horse, weights then being tied to his ankles to add extra emphasis to the questioning. Its main victims were men, but it is also believed to have been used for the punishment of prostitutes caught out of bounds in French army barracks!

Select Bibliography

Andrews, W., *Bygone Punishments* (Allan, 1931)
Benvenuti, F.F., *Episodes of the French Revolution* (Marshall, 1880)
Bryan, G., *Off With His Head* (Hutchinson, 1934)
Carlyle, T., *The French Revolution* (Ward Lock, 1837)
Clery, J., *Journal of Occurrences at the Temple Prison during Confinement of Louis XVI* (Paris, 1798)
Cooper, W.M., *History of the Rod* (Reeves, 1895)
Greer, D., *Incidents of Terror During the French Revolution* (Harvard University Press, 1935)
Howard, J., *State of the Prisons* (Dent, 1929)
Jephson, H., *The Real French Revolutionist* (Macmillan, 1899)
Kerr, W.B., *Reign of Terror 1793–4* (Toronto University Press, 1927)
Lenotre, G., *Guillotine and its Servants* (Hutchinson, 1908)
Lenotre, G., *Last Days of Marie Antoinette* (Hutchinson, 1907)
Lenotre, G., *Tribunal of the Terror* (Hutchinson, 1909)
Morton, J., *The Bastille Falls* (Longmans, Green, 1936)
Rose, J.H., *The Revolutionary & Napoleonic Era* (Cambridge University Press, 1907)
Sanson, H., *Memoirs of the Sansons* (Chatto & Windus, 1876)
Scott, G.R., *History of Torture Through the Ages* (Laurie, 1940)
Swain, J., *Pleasures of the Torture Chamber* (Douglas, 1931)
Symes, J.E., *The French Revolution* (Methuen, 1892)
Thompson, J.M., *English Witnesses of the French Revolution* (Blackwell, 1938)
Verdene, G., *La Torture* (R. Dorn, Paris, 1906)
Wheeler, H.F., *The French Revolution* (Jack, 1913)

Index